INSIGHT POCKET GUIDES

APA PUBLICATIONS

Nepal
50 miles / 80 km
CHINA
XIZANG ZIZHIQU
(TIBET)
NEPAL
INDIA
GREAT
HIMALAYA
RANGE
BYASRISHI HIMAL
CHANGLA HIMAL
SISNE HIMAL
KANJIROBA HIMAL
DHAULAGIRI HIMAL
ANNAPURNA HIMAL
GANESH HIMAL
LANGTANG HIMAL
KHUMBU HIMAL
SIWALIK
MAHABHARAT
(CHURIA)
RANGE
SINGALILA RANGE
Api 7132
Khiuri Khala 5990
Thari Patan 4543
Dhaulagiri 8167
Annapurna 8091
Manaslu 8163
7892 Himalchuli
Xixabangma 8012
6990 Dorjet Lapka
7145 Gauri Shankar
Cho Oyu 8201
Mount Everest 8848
8516 Lhotse
Baruntse 7129
8586 Kangchenjunga
6482 Qilaguganishan
Samuyishankou Pass 5526
Angden Pass 5642
Changlapod Pass 5572
Langtang Nat.l Park
Sagarmatha Nat.l Park
Mckalu Barun Nat.l Park
Tiger Tops Karnali Lodge & Tented Camp
Tharu Safari Resort
Tiger Tops Jungle Lodge
Katmandhu
Lagechi
Pulan
Nakechake
Maquanhe
Zhongba
Bubuduo
Teladuomu
Suluchi
Lingekeke
Saga
Lage
Angren
Raka Zangbo
Lingu
Lazhe
Mustang
Zongga
Yarlung Zangbo (Brahmaputra)
Sajia
Tingri
Xêgar
Dobzha
Jilong
Karta
Pithoragarh
Kali
Seti
Talkot
Dandeldhura
Silgarhi
Jumla
Tila
Bheri
Dailekh
Jajarkot
Dhangarhi
Puranpur
Mailani
Katarnian Ghat
Kumbher
Sallyan
Bijauri
Piuthan
Baglung
Bari
Pokhara
Kunchha
Gorkha
Bandipur
Makaising
Kali Gandaki
Tansen
Butwal
Narayani
Narayanghat
Bharatpur
Thankot
Patan
Bhaktapur
Hetauda
Amlekhganj
Ramechhap
Sun Kosi
Okhaldhunga
Sindhulimadi
Bhojpur
Arun
Taplejung
Terhathum
Dhankuta
Darjiling (Darjeeling)
Ilam
Dharan Bazar
Shiliguri
Udaypur
Bairia
Bagmati
Janakpur
Sirha
Sapt Kosi
Rajbiraj
Biratnagar
Kishanganj
Forbesganj
Nirmali
Madhubani
Kamla
Darbhanga
Samastipur
Purnia
Sitamarhi
Motihari
Birganj
Raxaul
Bettiah
Harnatanr
Bagaha
Gopalganj
Gandak
Siwan
Muzaffarpur
Hajipur
Nautanwa
Bhairahawa
Pharenda
Padrauna
Gorakhpur
Deoria
Maunath Bhanjan
Nepalganj
Lakhimpur
Sarda
Girwa
Bahraich
Balrampur
Sitapur
Hardoi
Gonda
Colonelganj
Sandila
Bara Banki
Basti
Faizabad
Ghaghara (Gogra)
Tanda
Lucknow
Kanpur
Unnao
Haidargarh
Ganga (Ganges)
Rae Bareli
Sultanpur
Gomati
Fatehpur
Yamuna
Jaunpur

Welcome!

This book is designed to bring you the best of Nepal. Locally based author Lisa Choegyal has created a series of 22 tailor-made itineraries (three full-day tours linking some of the country's outstanding highlights, 14 other half- and full-day tours, and five excursions) to help visitors get to grips with this enchanting country as quickly and easily as possible. Due attention is given to the three great Durbar Squares of Kathmandu, Patan and Bhaktapur, and the famous shrines of Bodhnath, Pashupatinath and Swayambhunath, but the book also takes a step further to less-trodden corners of the Kathmandu Valley – to the distant towns of Kirtipur and Panauti, the temples of Changu Narayan and Chandeshwari, and the stupa of Namo Buddha. The five excursions take you to the rivers, mountains and jungles outside the Kathmandu Valley.

Many of the itineraries can be done on foot or by hiring a bicycle, but some days you will need to arrange a car. Have a guide to help interpret the complexities of culture – for at least part of the time. At the same time do not be afraid to stray and explore on your own. The constant action in the streets, the clarity of light and the vibrant colours of the Kathmandu Valley enchant at every turn. The Nepalese captivate with their gentle charm and also their faith and traditions. Daily worship at shrines is part of life. Look, and you'll see the brass trays of offerings and the vermilion tika on a forehead.

Lisa Choegyal first came to Nepal over 20 years ago. Trekking in the Annapurnas, she became fascinated with Kathmandu and was enticed to the lowland jungles of Chitwan. 'I have lived here ever since and feel privileged that life has worked out this way for me,' she says. Lisa now works as director of Nepal's largest adventure travel group.

C O N T E N T S

History & Culture

Nepal's Highlights

These three full-day itineraries link the essential highlights of Kathmandu Valley.

Pick & Mix Itineraries

For visitors with particular interests we have created 10 optional itineraries.

Pages 2/3: forest below Annapurna II

Day Trips

Four easy day trips from Kathmandu.

Excursions

Five longer excursions for visitors with more time.

Pages 8/9: masked dancers, Hanuman Palace

Eating Out & Shopping

Calendar of Events

Practical Information

Maps

History & Culture

Nepal has long intrigued outsiders with fables of Lost Horizons and Shangri-Las. Shrouded in mystery until a recently as the 1950s when its borders were first opened to foreigners, Nepal has an astonishing diversity of terrain for such a small country. In just one day the organized visitor can fly amidst the world's highest mountains, browse amongst some of the world's most beautiful temples and ride elephants in the tall grasslands of the jungles.

A landlocked rectangle that curves along the line of the central Himalaya, Nepal is 553 miles (885km) long and from 90–150 miles (145–240km) wide. The stupendous heights of the white Himalaya, the 'Abode of the Gods', dominate the country and its culture. Eight of the 10 highest mountains in the world are within or on Nepal's borders, including the highest, Mount Everest, at 29,028ft (8,848m).

Massive rivers plunge through Himalayan gorges as they race from the high Tibetan plateau through the Mahabharat, or middle hills, irrigating the ochre-red terraces, then slowing through the fertile farmlands of the Terai and hardwood forests of the Si-

Kathmandu Valley with Ganesh Himal

walik (Churia) hills before eventually draining into the mighty River Ganges.

Entirely mountainous except for the narrow strip of the Terai along its southern border, Nepal's climates range from the alpine sub-zero temperatures of the highlands to the tropical heat of the Terai lowlands. Squeezed, physically and politically, between the vastness of China and India, Nepal's 19 million people live in a country roughly the size of England or New Zealand. They are a homogenous mix of cultures and customs and nowhere can this be better appreciated than in the Kathmandu Valley.

Valley of Plenty

Situated between the Great Himalayan and the Mahabharat ranges and located almost in the centre of Nepal, the broad fertile acres of the Valley of Kathmandu is the obvious choice for its capital. Covering an area of 220 sq miles (570 sq km), the Valley today supports a population of nearly one million people. The alluvial floor is very suitable for growing rice, the staple diet of the Nepalese, and it is well irrigated by the Bagmati River. At an altitude of 4,400ft (1,350m) above sea level, few capital cities enjoy such a clement climate with an unusual amount of sunshine and mean temperatures pleasantly varying between 10°–36°C (50°–97°F).

Pashupatinath Temple

Agriculture plays an important role in the daily life of the inhabitants and the changing cycle of the seasons are marked with the intense greens and yellows of cereal crops, the golden heaps of rice and the vivid reds of chillies. Natural wonders arrest the visitor at every turn in the Kathmandu Valley. Rivers and streams interlace the landscape, the brick red villages cling to ridges to preserve precious land and even from the bustling centres of the cities it is possible to catch a glimpse of the snowcapped peaks of the majestic Himalaya against the intensely blue sky. In addition, the most vibrant element of all, the people of Nepal and their kaleidoscope of culture.

Crossroads of Culture

Nowhere in the world can one find the same concentration of culture, art and tradition that co-exist in the Kathmandu Valley. Isolated by the Himalayan barrier to the north and malarial swamps to the south, Kathmandu Valley is a crucible of culture distilled from

A Terai wedding procession

centuries of travellers, traders, artists and artisans on their way between the ancient civilizations of China and India. The diversity of the people is immediately visible in the faces of the colourfully-clad crowds who cram the medieval streets of the old cities. The richness of the heritage can be measured in the tangle of temples, shrines, stupas and palaces, one more gloriously adorned than the next.

Kathmandu is a true cultural crossroads for the more than 30 different ethnic groups who live in the hills and lowland Terai of Nepal, a mosaic that embraces both Aryan and Mongol races, several religions and as many languages and traditions as there are peoples. In addition to the Sanskrit-based official language, Nepali, there are as many as 36 different languages, and many more dialects.

People come to the Kathmandu Valley on holy pilgrimages, to celebrate a special festival or to trade and barter in the bazaars. Many of the hill people still consider the Kathmandu Valley to be 'Nepal'. Thronging the streets you may see people from the north of Tibetan descent, Tamangs or 'horsemen', and the Sherpas of international mountain climbing fame. From all through the middle hills come Rais, Limbus, Gurungs Magars and Thakalis and the ubiquitous Brahmans and Chhetris, the high caste warriors. From the Terai come the aboriginal Tharus and Majhis, and many people of Indian origin. The early inhabitants of the Kathmandu Valley, the Newars, are one of the oldest of the ethnic groups, with a language so unusual its origins are still debated.

Sealed for centuries from Westerners, a common denominator of the myriad people of Nepal is their national pride and fierce independence, derived perhaps from the fact that Nepal has never been colonised, unlike so many Asian neighbours. Politeness is rated very highly by Nepalis, and to avoid offence remember this and keep any opinions you may have on controversial or political subjects to yourself. You will see portraits everywhere of the King and he is respected as a deity in Nepal.

Every Breath a Prayer

It is easy to believe that there are more gods than people in Kathmandu. The fusion of faith found uniquely in the Valley may be theologically bewildering but it is necessary to understand something of the religion to appreciate its role in the day to day life of the Nepali people.

It is often hard to distinguish between the two main spiritual currents of Hinduism and Buddhism, especially when they are interwoven with the exotica of Tantrism against a background of animistic cults retained from the distant past. As a very general rule, both Hindu and Buddhist temples may take the pagoda form, the difference is that the *shikara*-style temples are Hindu and the white-dome stupas are Buddhist.

The Hindu pantheon of gods include many colourful characters and fanciful stories. Many of these gods and goddesses appear in different guises under different names, which can be confusing to the visitor. Hardly a week passes without a festival, and daily offerings of flower petals, rice and vermilion powder on a brass tray are proffered in *puja* (to renew communion with the deities particularly relevant to one's own particular problems or circumstances) at the many hundreds of different shrines. Ritual sacrifice, whether as a blessing, initiation or as part of a festival, is always performed using a male animal, invariably a chicken, goat or buffalo. Sacrifice is a cornerstone of worship in Nepal's Hindu religion.

Many of Kathmandu's Newars are Buddhist, but will recognize Hindu gods in different forms and the same is true vice versa; Hindus regard the Buddha as an incarnation of Vishnu. It has been said that if one asks a Newar if he is Hindu or Buddhist, he will reply, 'Yes'. The question is meaningless and implies an exclusive choice which is completely foreign to the scope of the Newar's religious experience. The mixing of the two religions, plus the influence of Tantrism (*see below*), has added to the proliferation of cults, deities and celebrations.

Although political leaders have always been Hindu, Buddhism since its emergence in the 6th century, has been tolerated. In the centuries following the life of the Buddha in India, many doctrinal disputes arose, leading to various schisms in the philosophy. Most important was the break between the Theravada school, which today is dominant in Southeast Asia and Sri Lanka, and the Mahayana school, which spread north to Tibet. Tibetan or Mahayana Buddhism became highly developed in the remote vastness of the Tibetan plateau where it absorbed the original shamanisitic *Bon* faith. The followers of the four main sects of Mahayana Buddhism acknowledge the Dalai Lama as their spiritual leader. Tibetan Buddhism now thrives in Nepal's atmosphere of religious tolerance. Many new monasteries have been built at Bodhnath and Swayambhunath, and Buddha's birthplace at Lumbini is being developed for visitors.

One cannot speak of religions in Nepal without touching on the practice of Tantrism, a legacy of the pre-Buddhist medieval cultures of India which has been

Fine new silk and brocade thangka

largely eliminated elsewhere, thanks to the Moslem conquest, the influence of the British Raj and modern secularisation. Tantra is a Sanskrit word, referring to the basic warp of threads in weaving. Literally, Tantrism reiterates the Buddhist philosophy of the essential interweaving of all things and actions. It expanded the realm of Hindu gods, cults and rites and created within Buddhism a major trend called Vajrayana, the 'Path of the Thunderbolt', which reached great importance in Nepal, often finding expression in esoteric practices. The numerous Tantric gods are represented in human and animal forms, often with multiple hands and legs symbolizing the omnipresence and omnipotence of the divine. Many of these deities have a terrifying appearance, like forbidding Bhairav, bloodthirsty Kali or ambivalent Shiva, who in the Tantric pantheon is both creator and destroyer.

With such diversity, religious tolerance within Nepal is of the essence. Over the centuries, all the masterpieces of art produced by the great civilizations of the Kathmandu Valley are almost entirely religious in character, whether architecture, sculpture, woodcarving, metalwork, literature, music or dance. The marvellous legacy left by the early Newar artists and craftsmen is all inspired by their gods. No visitor can fail to be impressed by the wealth to be found literally lying around, the heritage of previous generations. The creative and turbulent history of the country explains many apparent conundrums.

The Legend of the Lake

In the distant dawn of unrecorded time when deities mingled with mortals the Valley of Kathmandu was a turquoise lake on which floated a white lotus flower from which emanated an awesome flame. Wishing to worship the flame more closely, the Buddhist patriarch Manjushri came from his mountain retreat in China and sliced the restraining Valley wall with his sacred sword so that the lotus might settle on what is now the hill of Swayambhunath.

A Hindu version of the story is that Krishna released the waters by hurling a thunderbolt at the Valley wall. Whatever the fiction, the fact is geologists confirm the Kathmandu Valley was once under water and the Chobar gorge is not only as narrow as a blade but below it, enshrined in a temple, is a stone that some believe to be Krishna's thunderbolt.

The evocative mythology of early Nepal gradually dissolves as, after several successive waves of hazy Tibeto-Burman migrants, the dynasty of Kirati kings gradually comes into historic focus in the seventh or eighth century BC. These apparently fierce tribal people invaded from the east and may have been the Kiriaths of Old Testament Babylon. Buddha was born as Prince Siddhartha Gautama in Lumbini in south Nepal during the reign of the 28 Kirati kings – the actual date of 543BC is disputed. Two centuries later the great Indian emperor Ashoka embraced Buddhism and converted his empire. He visited Lumbini, raised the engraved column and is believed to

Boats on Phewa Lake

have visited the Kathmandu Valley and had the Ashoka stupas built in Patan, though there is no actual proof.

Licchavi Legacy

When the Kiratis had succumbed to the Licchavi invasion from India in about AD300, the first golden age of Nepalese art flourished and stone sculptures survive today as a testament to the skill of their craftsmen. The oldest inscription in the Valley, AD464, is etched on a stone pillar at Changu Narayan, confirming King Manadeva I as a monarch of considerable talents, responsible for expanding his empire both to the east and west. The Licchavis also laid down the hierarchical structure of Nepaliese society, according to the Hindu caste system.

The three Thakuri dynasties began in AD602 with the ascent of King Amsuvarman, who married his sister to an Indian prince and his daughter, Bhrikuti, to Tibet's powerful King Tsrong-tsong Gompo. Bhrikuti is believed to have taken, as part of her dowry, the begging bowl of the Buddha. Her role in converting Tibet to Buddhism has made her a legendary figure, reincarnated as the Green Tara.

The Thakuri dynasties inaugurated the three great festivals of Indrajatra, Krishna Jayanti and the Machhendranath Jatras and it was during their time that the Kasthamandap or 'Pavilion of Wood' was constructed from a single tree, giving Kathmandu its name. This period lasted until 1200 and is termed Nepal's 'Dark Ages' as so little else is known of this time of obscure turmoil.

Marvellous Mallas (1274–1769)

The Malla kings controlled Nepal from the 13th to 18th centuries during a predominantly stable age of peace and plenty. It was the Malla kings who established the custom of being considered incarnations of Vishnu, as are the present Shah rulers. They adopted the Taleju Bhawani from South India as the royal goddess of Nepal. Although they were strict Hindus, they were tolerant of Buddhism which was widespread among the people, especially in its Tantric form. They developed the familiar compact villages seen today in the Valley using brick and tiles for the first time and clustered

King Bupathindra Malla at Bhaktapur

together to preserve limited arable land and as protection against bandits.

The Mallas survived a stormy period of earthquakes and the brief Moslem invasion of 1336. By the early 15th century they had introduced Newari as the court language and chosen Bhaktapur as their capital. A renaissance of art and culture flourished, laying the foundations of what we see today.

The dividing of the Valley in 1482 into three separate kingdoms, Kathmandu, Patan (Lalitpur) and Bhaktapur (Bhadgaon), no doubt encouraged each to compete with the next to glorify their palaces and temples, but led eventually to the downfall of their dynasty.

Shah Supremacy (1723–1846)

Political rivalries amongst the divided city-states led to their demise. The opportunity was seized by the King of Gorkha, then a principality situated halfway between Kirtipur and Pokhara, and which had been growing in strength under the dynamic leadership of King Prithvi Narayan Shah. After 10 years of preparation from his fort at Nuwakot, the founder of modern Nepal took Kathmandu and Patan by force in 1768 and Bhaktapur and Kirtipur yielded to him in 1769 by trickery and intrigue. The Valley was unified and he established Kathmandu as his capital. King Prithvi Narayan Shah and his descendants consolidated and expanded the new empire until it stretched from Kashmir to Sikkim, double its present size.

This led to inevitable conflicts with neighbours and the Chinese were eventually called in by the Tibetans to curb Nepal's expansionist ambitions to the north. An agreement was reached in 1792 which forced Nepal to desist.

A full-scale war with British India lasted from 1814 to 1816 and ended in the Treaty of Friendship, signed at Segauli, which shrank the borders to their present size and established a permanent British presence in Kathmandu. Brian Hodgeson was not the first European to visit the fabled Valley. The first British envoy, William Kirkpatrick, had visited in 1792 with regard to the disputes with Tibet, and the Italian Capuchins had been permitted a mission as early as 1730.

There is an interesting footnote to this period. The gallantry the Gorkha soldiers displayed in the 1816 conflict so impressed the British that they enlisted them into the British Indian Army. Even today the Gurkhas, as they are now called, are recognised as outstanding soldiers by the British and Indians.

Rana Rule (1846–1951)

In 1846, taking advantage of palace intrigues, the Kot Massacre was staged by the shrewd and enterprising Jung Bahadur Rana, who designated himself as prime minister, and later 'maharajah', with powers superior to those of the sovereign. He made his office hereditary, establishing a unique line of succession that went first to brothers and only then to sons. Ruthlessly suppressing all opposi-

Pokhara – boats on Phewa Lake

tion, he took the highly unusual step of traveling to Europe and was much impressed with Queen Victoria and the fashions of the day. On his return, he launched a frivolous vogue of neo-classical palaces, and ladies of the court arranged their *saris* to look like crinolines.

In all other respects, however, travel remained limited to a privileged few and foreigners were treated with extreme distrust.

It was only after King Tribhuvan managed, with help from India, to regain the royal powers in the almost-bloodless coup of early 1951 that Nepal opened its doors to the outside world. In 1953 Edmund Hillary and Sherpa Tenzing Norgay climbed Mount Everest – the news reached London on the eve of Queen Elizabeth's coronation. In the next decade the 'hippies' discovered the joys of Kathmandu Valley and settled in – until revised visa laws sent them on their way.

Despite early intentions, it was not until 1959 that Tribhuvan's son, King Mahendra, established a constitution that provided for a parliamentary system of government. The first general election in Nepal's history took place over several months in that year but the experiment with democracy was short-lived and ended in 1960 with the King taking back power. The 1962 constitution established the *panchayat* system, an administrative and legislative system culminating in an indirectly-elected national legislature, with the prime minister and cabinet appointed by the King.

King Mahendra died in 1972, and was succeeded by his son, the youthful King Birendra, who declared as his goal the improvement of the standard of living of his people. A referendum in 1980 reconfirmed the people's support of the monarchy and King Birendra, but by April 1990 popular dissatisfaction with the lack of reforms and corrupt officials erupted into demonstrations and riots in Kathmandu. The ban on the multi-party system was lifted, a democratic constitution was announced in November, 1990 and a general election held in May, 1991.

Nepal Today

King Birendra Bir Bikram Shah Dev today heads the only Hindu kingdom in the world. He is faced with some Himalayan sized problems, bringing his country into the 21st century to reach his goal of providing basic needs to the people by the year 2000. The population is increasing at the annual rate of 2.6 percent and rural poverty remains the chief problem. Foreign aid is a large component in Nepal's development budget and the nation's precarious position as a Himalayan buffer state between India and China may still be its best guarantee of survival, a foreign policy unchanged for centuries.

Historical Highlights

8th century BC–AD 300 The history of the eastern Kiriath kings are inextricably interwoven with legend.

AD300–700 The first golden age of Nepalese arts flourish in the Licchavi dynasty. The Valley's earliest stone inscription describes Nepal's first great historical figure, King Manadeva I. Leaving a legacy of superb stone sculptures, the Licchavis instigate the tradition of a hierarchical Hindu caste society.

AD602–1200 The "Dark Ages" of turmoil under the Tha-kuris, probably from northern India. Princess Bhrikuti of Nepal marries King Tsrong-tsong Gompo of Tibet and is deified as the Green Tara for converting him and Tibet to Buddhism, along with her Chinese co-wife, the White Tara.

1200 King Ari-deva assumes the title Malla, and sets up a new, highly-accomplished dynasty. The Mallas bring riches and recognition to Nepal, reinforce the caste system and establish the villages familiar to us today.

1336 The Mallas survive a raid by the Sultan of Bengal. By the 15th century a renaissance flourishes and many great buildings, fine woodcarving and powerful sculpture seen today belong to this period.

1482 King Yaksha Malla dies; the Valley is divided and ruled as three city-states: Kathmandu, Patan (Lalitpur) and Bhaktapur (Bhad-gaon). Agriculture and cottage industries thrive but political rivalries fragment the empire.

1768 Prithvi Narayan Shah, ruler of Gorkha, conquers Kathmandu and Patan and takes Bhaktapur a year later, thus founding a united Nepal and the present Shah dynasty. Expansionist policies and conflicts of trading interests lead to clashes with Nepal's neighbours.

1792 Invasion by Chinese troops follows several wars with Tibet. Nepal has to pledge to desist from attacking Tibet and to pay tribute regularly to the Chinese emperor in Peking.

1816 'Treaty of Friendship' signed; ends two years of war with British India. Nepal's territory is cut in half to its present borders. A British representative is established in Kathmandu, the first and only Western envoy resident in Nepal.

1846 Jung Bahadur Rana takes advantage of palace intrigue to stage the 'Kot Massacre' and establishes the Rana regime of hereditary ruling prime ministers. The Ranas rule Nepal, virtually keeping the royal family prisoners for ceremonial and religious purposes.

1951 King Tribhuvan regains royal power, aided by recently independent India. Foreigners are now allowed into Nepal and two years later, Mount Everest is climbed.

1962 After an unsuccessful experiment with parliamentary rule, King Mahendra institutes the *panchayat* system of government.

1972 King Birendra succeeds to the throne on the death of his father, King Mahendra.

1980 A national referendum is called by King Birendra following unrest, and reaffirms the people's confidence in the *panchayat* system.

1990 Following demonstrations and riots, King Birendra on 8 April lifts the legal ban on political parties. The constitution of 9 November invests sovereignty in the people, guarantees human rights and introduces a parliamentary system with the King relegated to a constitutional monarch.

1991 The general election on 12 May is won by the Nepali Congress and Girija Prasad Koirala becomes Prime Minister.

1996 Coalition Cabinet with Prime Minister Sher Bahadur Deuba.

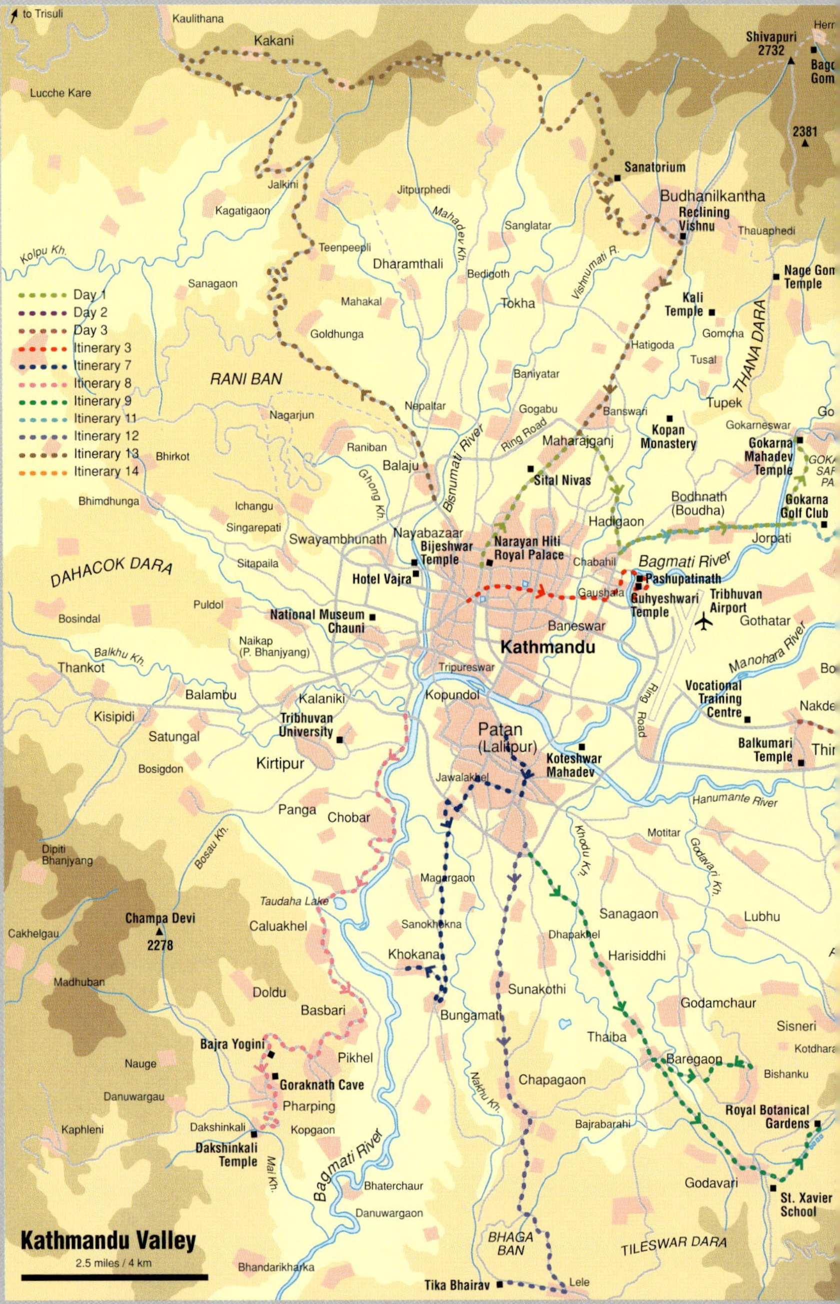

Kathmandu Valley
2.5 miles / 4 km
to Trisuli
Kaulithana
Kakani
Lucche Kare
Shivapuri
2732
2381
Sanatorium
Budhanilkantha
Reclining Vishnu
Thauaphedi
Jalkini
Jitpurphedi
Kagatigaon
Mahadev Kh.
Sanglatar
Vishnumati R.
Kolpu Kh.
Teenpeepli
Dharamthali
Bedigoth
Sanagaon
Mahakal
Tokha
Nage Gomba Temple
Kali Temple
Gomcha
Hatigoda
Tusal
THANA DARA
Goldhunga
Baniyatar
RANI BAN
Nepaltar
Gogabu
Banswari
Tupek
Nagarjun
Ring Road
Kopan Monastery
Gokarneswar
Maharajganj
Gokarna Mahadev Temple
Raniban
Balaju
Bhirkot
Ghong Kh.
Bisnumati River
Sital Nivas
Gokarna Golf Club
Bhimdhunga
Ichangu
Bodhnath (Boudha)
Hadigaon
Singarepati
Swayambhunath
Nayabazaar
Jorpati
Bijeshwar Temple
Narayan Hiti Royal Palace
Chabahil
Bagmati River
DAHACOK DARA
Sitapaila
Hotel Vajra
Pashupatinath
Gaushala
Guhyeshwari Temple
Tribhuvan Airport
Puldol
Bosindal
National Museum Chauni
Gothatar
Baneswar
Naikap (P. Bhanjyang)
Kathmandu
Balkhu Kh.
Thankot
Tripureswar
Manohara River
Vocational Training Centre
Balambu
Kalaniki
Kopundol
Ring Road
Nakde
Kisipidi
Tribhuvan University
Patan (Lalitpur)
Satungal
Balkumari Temple
Koteshwar Mahadev
Bosigdon
Kirtipur
Jawalakhel
Hanumante River
Panga
Chobar
Khodu Kh.
Motitar
Dipiti Bhanjyang
Godavari Kh.
Bosau Kh.
Magargaon
Taudaha Lake
Sanagaon
Lubhu
Champa Devi
2278
Caluakhel
Sanokhokna
Cakhelgau
Dhapakhel
Harisiddhi
Khokana
Madhuban
Sunakothi
Doldu
Godamchaur
Basbari
Bungamati
Sisneri
Thaiba
Kotdhara
Bajra Yogini
Pikhel
Baregaon
Nauge
Bishanku
Goraknath Cave
Chapagaon
Danuwargau
Nakhu Kh.
Pharping
Royal Botanical Gardens
Kaphleni
Dakshinkali
Bajrabarahi
Kopgaon
Dakshinkali Temple
Bagmati River
Mai Kh.
Godavari
Bhaterchaur
St. Xavier School
Danuwargaon
BHAGA BAN
TILESWAR DARA
Bhandarikharka
Tika Bhairav
Lele
Day 1
Day 2
Day 3
Itinerary 3
Itinerary 7
Itinerary 8
Itinerary 9
Itinerary 11
Itinerary 12
Itinerary 13
Itinerary 14

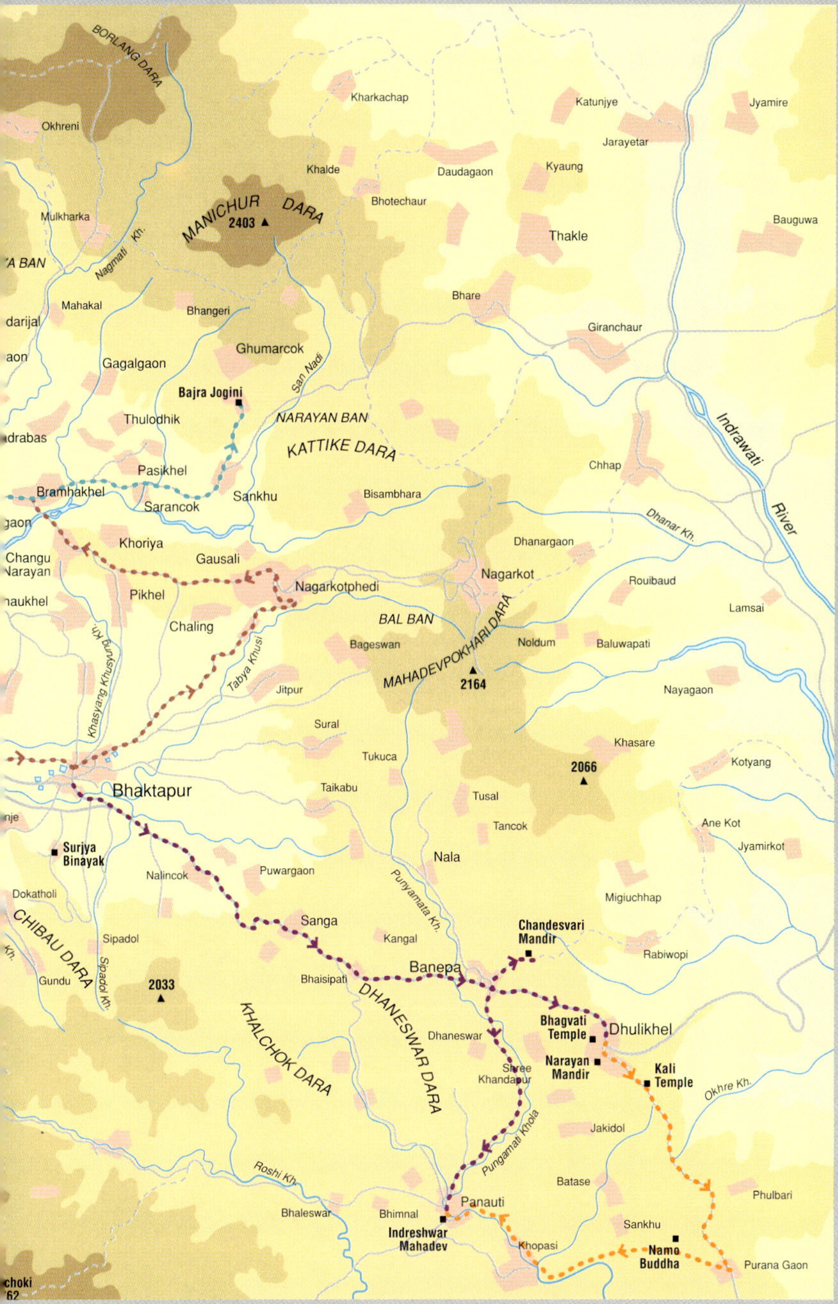

BORLANG DARA
Okhreni
Kharkachap
Katunjye
Jyamire
Jarayetar
Khalde
Daudagaon
Kyaung
Bhotechaur
MANICHUR DARA
2403
Mulkharka
Nagmati Kh.
Thakle
Bauguwa
A BAN
Mahakal
Bhangeri
Bhare
darijal
Giranchaur
Ghumarcok
aon
Gagalgaon
San Nadi
Bajra Jogini
NARAYAN BAN
Thulodhik
Indrawati River
drabas
KATTIKE DARA
Chhap
Pasikhel
Bramhakhel
Sankhu
Bisambhara
Sarancok
gaon
Dhanar Kh.
Dhanargaon
Khoriya
Changu Narayan
Gausali
Nagarkot
Rouibaud
Nagarkotphedi
naukhel
Pikhel
Lamsai
BAL BAN
Chaling
MAHADEVPOKHARI DARA
Bageswan
Noldum
Baluwapati
Khasyang Khusyang Kh.
Tabya Khusi
2164
Jitpur
Nayagaon
Sural
Khasare
Tukuca
Kotyang
2066
Bhaktapur
Taikabu
Tusal
nje
Ane Kot
Tancok
Jyamirkot
Surjya Binayak
Nala
Nalincok
Puwargaon
Punyamata Kh.
Dokatholi
Migiuchhap
Sanga
CHIBAU DARA
Chandesvari Mandir
Sipadol
Kangal
Rabiwopi
Kh.
Banepa
Gundu
2033
Sipadol Kh.
Bhaisipati
DHANESWAR DARA
KHALCHOK DARA
Bhagvati Temple
Dhulikhel
Dhaneswar
Narayan Mandir
Shree Khandapur
Kali Temple
Okhre Kh.
Jakidol
Pungamati Khola
Roshi Kh.
Batase
Phulbari
Panauti
Bhaleswar
Bhimnal
Sankhu
Indreshwar Mahadev
Khopasi
Namo Buddha
Purana Gaon
choki
62

Day Itineraries

Everyone arriving in Kathmandu is exhilarated, either by the clear sparkling views, the friendly people or the thrill of being in a city of which they have long dreamed. These first three days are designed to crystalise that excitement.

Day 1

Kathmandu Durbar Square and Bodhnath

Wander in the medieval magic of the Kathmandu Durbar Square. Walk through the bazaars of Asan and Indrachowk. Lunch in the garden at Mike's Breakfast. Grab a cab to Chabahil and linger at the stupa of Bodhnath, one of the great sights of the Valley. Drive through the countryside to the Gokarna Mahadev temple.

Looking west across the Kathmandu Valley

Although Nepalis live with the light, the morning mist in the winter makes it pointless leaving your hotel until 9.30am, after a leisurely breakfast. Spring and early autumn are more inspiring for an early start.

From the **Tundhikhel**, the central parade ground that separates the new city from the old, walk under the arch and up **New Road**, so-called as it was rebuilt after the terrible earthquake of 1934. It is lined with shops selling imported goods, drugs and jewels but they do not open early.

At the top you enter a different world. On your left is forgotten **Freak Street**, the abandoned hangout of the 1960s hippies and flower children, and nearby is the raised brick platform of **Basantapur**, formerly the home of royal elephants.

Ahead is the **Kathmandu Durbar Square**, the hub of the old city at the crossroads of diagonal trade routes. Founded by the Licchavi kings in the 8th century, this profusion of over 50 temples and monuments is a living museum to the glorious Malla dynasty architecture, with some additions by King Prithvi Narayan Shah and the Ranas.

You first encounter the **Kumari Bahal**

Kathmandu Durbar Square

(a) Kumari Bahal
(b) Temple of Narayan
(c) Kasthamandap
(d) Ashok Binayak
(e) Shiva Temple
(f) Shiva-Parvati Temple House
(g) King Pratap Malla
(h) Degu Taleju Temple
(i) Basantapur Tower
(j) Hanuman Dhoka
(k) Nasal Chowk
(l) Mohan Chowk
(m) Sundari Chowk
(n) Basantapur Tower
(o) Kirtipur Tower
(p) Lalitpur Tower
(q) Bhaktapur Tower
(r) Lohan Chowk
(s) Pancha Mukhi Hanuman
(t) Jagnnath Temple
(u) Gopinath Mandir
(v) Taleju Temple
(w) Tarana Devi Mandir

LAINCHAUR
Thayabju Restaurant
Tiger Tops Mountain Travel
Dairy Milk Scheme
Lekhnath Marg
Paknajol
Bhagwan Bahal
Kaldhara
Thamel
Gorkha Palace Restaurant
Dept. of Immigration
Narayan Hiti Royal Palace
Narayan Mandir
Tukucha
Indreni-Lhutiajima
Keshar Library
Saarc Headquarters
Bahadur Bhawan
Kanti Path
Tiger Tops Adv. Travel Nepal
Narayan Hiti
Swiss Air
Seto Durbar
Dhobicaur
KWABAHAL
British Council
CHETREPATI
Kwa Bahal
Musya Bahal
German Embassy
Ghar E Kabab Restaurant
Mike's Breakfast
Lal Durbar
Sun Kosi Restaurant
River
Swachapu Ganesh
JYATHA
Lufthansa Thai Int.
Air France,
British Airways
THAHITI
Chusya Bahal
KAMALACHI
Nyata Ganesh
TENGAL
Kathe Simbhu
Dhoka Bahal
KLM
Kamaladi
Royal Nepal Academy
Mosque
NAGHAL
Raktakali
Ikha Narayan
Bhandra Char Restaurant
BANGEMURHA
Vishnumati (Bisnumati)
NARDEWI
BHO TAHITI
Rani Pokhari
KILAGAL
ASAN TOL
Kamaladi Ganesh
Annapurna Pith
Clock Tower
Kankeswari
YATKHA
Jana Bahal
Itu Bahal
French Cultural Centre
KHEL TOL
Yatkha Bahal
Bead Market
Bagh Bazaar
Akash Bhairav
MAHABUDDHA
RATNA
INDRACHOWK
PYAPHAL
MAKHANTOL
Durbar
Mahabuddha
Taleju
Khu Bahal
Hanuman Dhoka
Bir Hospital
Maru Bahil
PARK
Ram Shah Path
Bus Station
MARU
Mahakala
Durbar Square
Supermarket
Kasthamandap
YENGAL
BHIMSENTHAN
Tourist Inf. Centre
Ganga Path
New Road
Military Hospital
City Hall
Basantapur
Adko Narayan
JHOCHE
Nepal Bank
Dharma Path
Te Bahal
Bhrikutimandap Marg
Bhimsen Mandir
TEBAHAL
OIKAMUGAL
Harisankar
Ranmukteswar
OMBAHAL
Tundhikhel
EXHIBITION GROUND
Goethe Institute
Marg
Tankeswari
JAISIDEWAL
Vegetable Market
Jaisi Dewal
General & Foreign Post Office
Bhimsen Tower
Duty Free Centre
GANABAHAL
Prithwi Path
Minister
Ram Chandra Narayan
Hari Bhawan
Martyr's Memorial
Bhadrakali
Kalimati
Machhendranath
Kanti Path
Prithwi Path
Hyumata Narayan
BRAMHATOL
HYUMATA
LAGANTOL
Bhote Bahal
Tukuca Khola
Valley View Hotel
Jagannath
Ram Shah Path
Supreme Court
National Stadium
Tripureswar Marg
National Archives
Teku Hospital
Central Telegraph Office
Teku
Pachali Bhairav
Tripureswar
Arniko Rajmarg
Siwalaya
Tripura Sundari
Juddha Ghat
Teku Masan
Bagmati River
Thapatha
Bluebird Supermarket
Rajghat
Kalamochan
Kopundole
Maternity Hospital
1
2
3
4
6
7
8
9
10
11
12
13
14
15

Gairi Dhara
Tangal
Police HQ
Maneswari
Narayancaur
Harigaon
Sita Bhawan
Siwa Mandir
Bhagwati
Sanu Gaucharan
Gyaneswar
Gyaneswar
Dhobi Khola
Chabahil
Candrabinayak
Chabahil Stupa
to Bodhnatz
Siphal
Deopatan
Pashupatinath
Bhuwaneswari
Bhandarkhal
Jayabageswari
Banakali
Ring Road
Bazaar
Maitidevi
Maiti Devi
Battisputali
Kalikasthan
Baneswar
Bagmati
Singha Durbar
Dhobi Khola
Dewkota Marg
Baneswar
Baneswar
Convention Centre
Hotels :
1 Ambassador
2 Annapurna
3 Blue Star
4 Crystal
5 Everest
6 Kathmandu Guest House
7 Malla
8 Manang
9 Mayalu
10 Mt. Makalu
11 Nook
12 Panorama
13 Siddharta
14 Star
15 Woodlands
Day 1
Itinerary 5
Kathmandu
400 m / 440 yds

Royal Palace window

on the left, the mid 18th-century temple of the **Kumari** or Living Goddess. The inner façades, like the main one, have beautifully carved windows and it is here that she can sometimes be persuaded to appear to her admirers. A virgin chosen from the Sakya clan of goldsmiths, the Kumari never leaves the sanctuary of her temple except when she is ceremoniously paraded in her chariot at the festival of Indrajatra, when even the King pays her homage.

Ahead, the **Kasthamandap** is at the entrance of the **Maru Tol**, the original Pavilion of Wood said to have been constructed from a single sacred tree, and from where Kathmandu gets its name. Originally a community centre it is now a temple dedicated to Gorakh-nath. Pause at the golden **Maru Ganesh** shrine, a monument of great importance and always very busy with devotees ensuring their safety before leaving on a journey. Rest on the nine steps of the **Shiva Temple** whilst admiring the crudely carved deities surveying the scene from the window of the **Shiva-Parvati Temple House**.

As you leave the main square, note the great drums on your left which are beaten during the worship of the **Degu Taleju** in her temple opposite. The north-facing door is panelled in silver and the 92-ft (28-m) high roof is capped with a very fine pinnacle. The proud statue of **King Pratap Malla**, who is responsible for much of this glory, is set high on a pillar opposite. Before you move on, notice the large golden mask of **Bhairav** erected in 1796, normally kept screened from view except during the festival of Indrajatra when chhang or local beer pours from his mouth and down the throats of the excited crowd.

Now you are in second square that is dominated by the towering **Taleju Temple**, the royal deity, whose inner sanctum can only be entered by the King. Built in 1564 by Mahendra Malla, this used to be the highest structure in Kathmandu and at 121ft (37m) it was considered inauspicious to build higher.

Kathmandu Durbar Square at dusk

Vishnu as half-lion, half-man

The entrance to the sprawling old Royal Palace, the **Hanuman Dhoka Durbar**, is a brightly painted gate (open 10am–4pm, closed Tuesday), flanked by stone lions and guarded by the palace's namesake Hanuman, the monkey god, a red-smeared image which dates from 1672. Pass through the golden doors. There is much to explore within this series of superb courtyards, beautifully decorated and still used by the Royal family for ceremonies and special days.

Admire incomparable woodcarving, the King Tribhuvan museum in the **Nasal Chowk** and orient yourself from the nine-storey **Basantapur Tower**. The **Kirtipur Tower** has a domed copper roof, the **Bhaktapur Tower** is of an octagonal form and the **Lalitpur Tower** overlooks New Road. The towers were named after the towns that donated and built them in recognition of the unification of Nepal by King Prithvi Narayan Shah. The Hanuman Dhoka Durbar was extensively and carefully

restored by UNESCO for King Birendra's coronation in February, 1975, which had been delayed until the most auspicious day.

Leaving behind these great marvels of art and architecture, return to the square and turn right past the fearsome features of the much revered **Black Bhairav**, and shudder at the bloodshed in the **Kot**, the armoury where Jung Bahadur enacted his merciless coup in 1846 by murdering most of those in power. The half-buried **Garuda** at the entrance to **Makhan Tol** is evocative of former times and street levels. Leaving the Durbar Square, the road narrows through the bazaar heading in a northeasterly direction. There are many shrines, courtyards and shops to investigate as you jostle with colourfully-costumed people and honking rickshaws.

At **Indrachowk**, detour into the quaint **Bead Market** through the smallest of passages behind the house opposite the many-balconied **Akash Bhairav**. Sitting in their adjacent booths, the shopkeepers will twist and string together a bewildering array of multi-coloured glass beads to your specifications.

At the next junction, **Khel Tol**, step left through a small gate which leads you into the important **Seto Machhendranath Temple**, home of the guardian deity of Kathmandu, before continuing to the throng of **Asan Tol**. Be prepared as your senses are bombarded with sights, sounds and smells.

Keep walking straight ahead and you emerge from the bazaar at a square pond, **Rani Pokhari**, with a domed Shiva shrine in the middle, built in 1670 by King Pratap Malla to console his queen on the death of their son.

Cross the road, but not before noting where you can rent a bicycle, and head along **Jamal Tol** to **Durbar Marg**, the wide avenue where most of the travel agents and airlines are to be found. The **Narayan Hiti Royal Palace** is in front of you, named after

Indrachowk

the water spout found at the top of the street on the right.

Half-way up Durbar Marg, turn right under the Yak and Yeti Hotel arch. **Mike's Breakfast**, to whose peaceful garden you are heading for lunch, is down the first lane to your right. Order a fresh lime soda while you check the menu for the daily special or select from the generous quiches and iodine-cleansed salads.

When you feel refreshed, take a taxi or better still, arrange a hired car and head north past the Royal Palace up **Lazimpat** and **Maharajgunj**, the area where many foreign missions are found, past the two Princes' palaces to the **Ring Road**, which circles the city. This is not the most direct route to **Bodhnath** but it gives you a chance to gauge the size of the city and appreciate its rural nature. On a clear day the white peaks of **Ganesh Himal** and **Dorje Lakpa** can be seen across the rice fields and distant foothills.

Bodhnath Stupa

It is worth stopping at the stupa of **Chabahil**, one of the very earliest settlements in the Valley, now sitting rather dilapidated. Chabahil stupa is said to have been constructed from materials left over from Bodhnath.

To the west about 215yds (200m) is the beautiful Ganesh shrine of **Chandra Binayak** which is believed to cure diseases and injuries. A brass shrew waits for Ganesh, the helpful son of Shiva, atop a pillar in front of the shrine, resplendent under a modern light.

Spend time lingering at **Bodhnath**, the largest stupa in the Valley whose great dome rises out of the paddy fields against a brilliant blue sky with a backdrop of white Himalayan peaks. Shaped like a massive *mandala*, which is best discerned from the air, and decorated with strings of fluttering prayer flags, Bodhnath has always been a centre for trade with Tibet. The all-seeing eyes on the stupa follow Buddhist pilgrims from Tibet, Ladakh, Bhutan and the northern parts of Nepal as they circumambulate clockwise, spinning the embossed prayer wheels. Along the base of the great hemispherical stupa are a ring of 108 small inset images of the Buddha.

To get a glimpse of Buddhist life, explore the surrounding monasteries, many of which are newly built by Western as well as local donors. Bodhnath has become one of the most important Tibetan Buddhist centres in the world.

A charming legend obscures the ancient origins of Bodhnath. It is said that a girl called Kangma built the stupa. Having been banished from heaven by Indra for stealing flowers, she was reborn, as punishment, the daughter of a swineherd.

On earth she had four children, was widowed then managed to

make a fortune as a goose girl. She asked the king to give her as much land as the hide of a buffalo would cover, so that she could build a noble temple to the Buddha. The king agreed and the clever girl cut the hide into thin strips, joined them and stretched them out to encircle the land on which Bodhnath now stands.

Do not miss the shopping opportunities at the stalls and small shops that surround the stupa – trinkets, carpets and ethnic fabrics. Look out for the special little shop selling jackets and waistcoats, made from the wool cloth normally used by monks and trimmed with ribbon.You may want to stop for a refreshing lemon tea at the first-floor Stupa View Restaurant.

Drive on and when the forest of Gokarna comes into sight, turn left and follow the road that winds through the fields on its way to **Sundarijal**, one of the Valley's main water supplies. After about 3 miles (5km) you reach the little village of Gokarna.

The **Gokarna Mahadev** is on the right of the road, a beautifully restored triple-roofed shrine on the banks of the sacred Bagmati with superb carved roof struts. This was the first renovation project of the Kathmandu Valley Preservation Trust. At the **Gokarna Aunshi** festival in June or July, devotees whose fathers have died in the past year must come here and ritually bathe in the river. A particularly fine image of Parvati, Shiva's consort, is enshrined at the northwest corner, recently modestly garbed to shield her beauty.

After relaxing at your hotel, dine Nepali at the **Bhancha Ghar** restaurant (Tel: 225-172) in Kamaldi, where there are handicraft demonstrations, or at the Soaltee Oberoi's **Himalchuli** restaurant (Tel: 272-550) where you can enjoy an 8pm cultural show, staged every evening.

DAY 2

Bhaktapur to Panauti

Drive to the ancient city of Bhaktapur, then walk through the Durbar Square, the Taumadhi Square with the five-roofed Nyatapola Temple and the Dattatreya Square before driving on outside the Valley to the Dhulikhel Mountain Resort for lunch with a view. Return to Banepa and the Chandeshwari temple, with its extraordinary fresco of Bhairav. Then, a visit to the classic Newar town of Panauti and its important temples.

Arrange a car for the day and drive to **Bhaktapur**, also known by its old name of Bhadgaon. Leave it at the entrance to the **Durbar Square**. This most charming of the three Durbar Squares has the best preserved, 'medieval' character and immediately evident is the relative sparseness due to the destruction by the 1934 earthquake.

Opposite the gilded copper **Sun Dhoka** (Golden Gate), erected in 1753 and hailed as one of the greatest single pieces of Nepali art, is the lovely statue of **Bupathindra Malla** on his tall pillar of stone. Passing through the gate, walk left into the **Mul Chowk** and explore as far as you can before being stopped by guards from entering the sacred and richly ornamented **Taleju Chowk** and **Kumari Chowk**. You are permitted to see the sunken bathing pool known as the **Nag Pokhari**, with its beautiful gilded water spout.

Bhairav temple from the Nyatapola steps

Returning to the main square, notice the octagonal pavilion, the **Chayasilin Mandap**, which has taken three painstaking years to reconstruct from contemporary drawings, on its original plinth. Donated to the people of Nepal by Chancellor Kohl of Germany, the exquisite woodcarving is a tribute to today's craftsmen and the shameless steel girders a tribute to German technology.

Adjacent to the Sun Dhoka is the **Royal Palace of 55 Windows**, rebuilt after it was almost completely destroyed by the 1934 earthquake. Examine the **thangkas** in the rearranged **National Art Gallery**, which is in another part of the palace located through a gateway

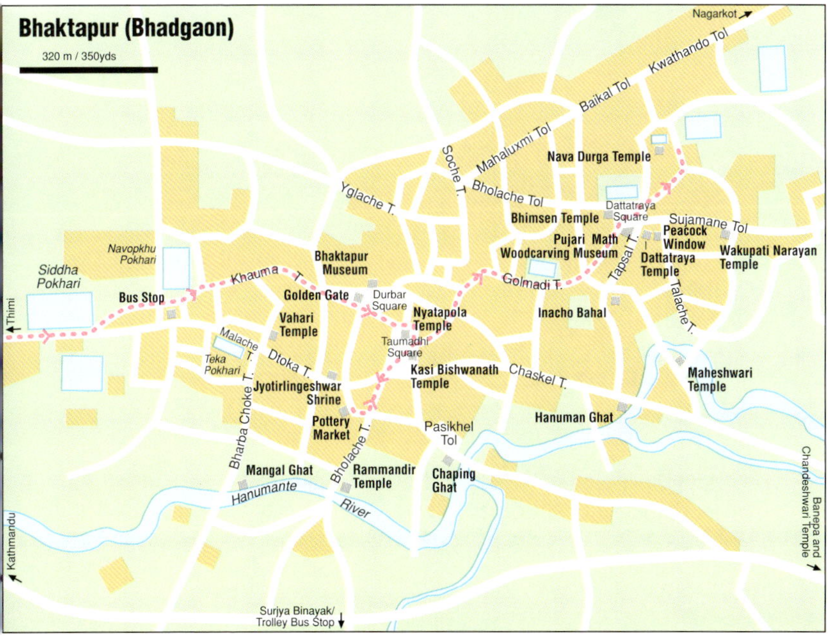

Decorated torana

flanked by Hanuman and Narsingh, the man-lion. Before you leave, note the **Sundari Chowk**, the ritual bathing courtyard of the Bhaktapur kings, no longer surrounded by any buildings.

Leave by the **Taumadhi Tol**, a narrow street leading down to the **Taumadhi Square**, lined with tempting shops selling **thangkas**, puppets and artefacts. On your left is the superb five-roofed **Nyatapola Temple** on its five plinths, one of the tallest in the Valley over 98ft (30m) high, dedicated to a mysterious Tantric goddess. Notice the pairs of guardians who flank the main staircase, each ten times stronger than the one below. Thus the Malla wrestlers on the bottom plinth are ten times as strong as ordinary men but only one tenth as powerful as the elephants above them, and so on. It is told that King Bupathindra Malla himself carried bricks for the building of the temple to inspire the locals.

At right angles is the earlier **Kasi Bishwanath Temple**, whose Bhairav is paraded at the frenetic annual Bisket festival at the Nepali New Year. Pause for a cup of Nepali chiya (tea brewed together with milk, sugar and spices) in the temple cafe and enjoy the busy life of the Square. The black saris edged in red are unique to the Newar women of Bhaktapur. Notice the jyapus, the Newari farmers, carrying their loads in two baskets strung on a pole across their shoulders. Only Newars use this method of carrying, all the other people of Nepal prefer to use the doko, or

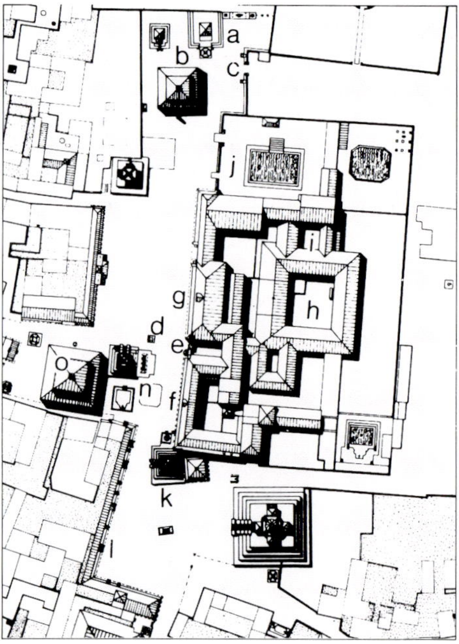

Bhaktapur Durbar Square

(a) gateway
(b) Rameshwar Temple dedicated to Shiva
(c) Temple dedicated to Durga
(d) Bhupatindra Malla
(e) Sun Dhoka
(f) Royal Palace
(g) National Art Gallery
(h) Taleju Chowk
(i) Kumari Chowk
(j) Sundari Chowk
(k) Dharmasala
(l) Tadhunchen Bahal
(m) Batsala Durga
(n) Pashupati Temple

basket, supported on their backs by a strap around their foreheads.

Detour south from here, if you wish, to the Pottery Market, then return and walk on down the brick paved streets, via the **Golmadi Tol**, past the little **Golmadi Ganesh Shrine** to the eastern part of Bhaktapur and the **Dattatraya Square**.

The **Dattatraya Temple** is the oldest in this area, as can be devised from its squat shape, not dissimilar to the Kasthamandap in Kathmandu. Considered to be one of the most important temples in the Valley, and serving as both a place of rest and a shrine, the front part (added later) houses the images of Dattatraya, honoured as Shiva's teacher.

Dhulikhel Mountain Resort

Down a side alley behind it is the famed (though somewhat overrated) **Peacock Window**. Do not miss the **Woodcarving Museum** nearby in the ancient priest's house, the **Pujari Math**, and formerly the headquarters of the German Bhaktapur Development Project which restored much of the city. Have the car meet you behind the **Nava Durga**, a rather sinister and highly revered temple that is the focus of the ritual masked dancing during festivals.

It is a very pleasant 45-minute drive through the countryside to the **Dhulikhel Mountain Resort** (Tel: 011-220031) for lunch on the road to Tibet. As you leave the Valley at the village of **Sanga**, pause to look back at the panoramic view. The Resort is several miles on past the town of Dhulikhel and do not be tempted to stop at any of the other hostelries. At the Dhulikhel Mountain Resort, perched high above the road, ask to eat outside in the garden to enjoy the mountain views. The marinated chicken kebab is excellent. If you are filled with energy, walk along the ridge for an hour or so above the resort to the little shrine beneath a big tree.

From Dhulikhel drive back down the road to Kathmandu and turn right (north) at the statue of King Tribhuvan in the middle of **Banepa**, a thriving town with many new buildings. Follow the road right and, if you have a genuine interest, call in at the **Banepa Adventist Hospital**. Any old clothes, medicines and donations are made excellent use of in this busy general hospital which serves an impressively large area.

Drive a little further, as far as you can, until the golden roof of the **Chandeshvari Mandir** comes into view on the edge of a steep gorge. The forest above here was believed to have been once full of demon beasts, and the goddess Parvati was called upon to slay their leader, Chand. The shrine was built in her honour and in the sanctum there is a fine image of Chandeshvari, the Master of the Slayer of Chand. The multi-coloured fresco of Bhairav is worth the trip here.

Brahmayani Temple, Panauti

Returning to the Banepa crossroads, the classic Newar town of **Panauti** is a 20-minute drive straight across, a settlement which is possibly pre-Licchavi in origin and a thriving trading town in Malla times. Leave the car at the confluence of the **Pungamati River** and visit the exquisite **Brahmayani Temple**, restored a few years ago by French experts. Cross by the suspension foot bridge and explore the scenic melange of ancient temples and *ghats*. There is a Krishna temple and several Shiva **lingums**.

Walk right to the magnificent **Indreshwar Mahadev**, one of the oldest existing temple structures with some of the earliest woodcarving to be found in Nepal. Founded as early as the 12th and 13th centuries, the carved wood roof struts are masterly in their elegant simplicity. A French project is restoring the earthquake damage suffered in 1988. Inside its walled courtyard, note the **Narayan Temple** opposite. Panauti is the end of your walk in *Itinerary 14, Pick & Mix*.

From Panauti it is less than an hour's journey back to Kathmandu. Indian kebabs, *tikas*, curries and sitar music at the **Ghar e Kebab** (Tel: 221-711) on Durbar Marg may appeal this evening or perhaps you would prefer Tibetan food at the **Sun Kosi Restaurant** (Tel: 226-520) in Kamaladi. Try the *thukpa*, a thick noodle soup, and fried *momos*, a delicious kind of ravioli popular with Tibetans.

DAY 3

A Walk to Changu Narayan

An early start by car via Thimi to Nagarkot, high on the rim of the Valley. Walk for about three hours part way down the hill along a ridge with views across the Valley, picnicking en route, to the wonderful temple of Changu Narayan. Ancient sculptures litter the courtyard and here is the earliest inscription in the Valley. An evening stroll in Chetrapati and Thamel with a European dinner at the Shangrila Hotel.

After an early breakfast, this morning you should leave by 8.30am with an arranged car for Nagarkot (up to 7,200ft/2,200m). Take something warm to wear, a packed lunch and a water bottle. Enjoy the old back road via **Thimi**, where the terracotta animals are

Nagarkot

sold by the roadside. Look out for the particularly engaging painted figures of the King and Queen. Turn off left behind Bhaktapur, past the 'industrial estate' which produces glazed pottery and handmade paper for UNICEF cards, available in the craft shops opposite the Himalaya Hotel in Patan.

The road to **Nagarkot** winds upward through fields and then through pine trees, and you can feel the temperature dropping as you climb. Identify the ridge along which you will be walking later by picking out the gold roofs of Changu Narayan on the left. The view of the receding tiers of blue-grey hills culminating in the white snows will be reward enough for the one-hour drive. On the way stop for refreshments with a view at the Tea House (Tel: 290-880). If the weather is really overcast, do not bother going all the way to the top.

Leave the car half way down the hill at the saddle where the ridge joins the road, making sure the driver understands where to meet you – by the teashop on the Sankhu Road below Changu. The first 20 minutes up through a pine plantation to the crest is the only uphill climb of the day! The walk is a leisurely, three-hour stroll along the ridge line with stunning views across the Valley to the high mountains. If you need reassurance, there is

Thimi pottery

always someone to ask the way. Note the traces of an old Rana irrigation system and the orange pumpkins and red chillies drying on the roofs. The glittering pinnacles of Changu Narayan tempt you on through charming Chhetri and Gurung villages. It is more peaceful to eat your picnic by the trail before you reach the village of Changu.

At the top of the main street is the superb temple complex of **Changu Narayan**, rebuilt in 1702 but with the Valley's earliest inscription etched on a pillar and dating its origins to AD464. Marvel at the treasury of priceless Licchavi sculptures of Vishnu and Garuda images, the statues of Bupathindra Malla in a gilded cage and the unusual brickwork on the platform. Changu Narayan has been designated a World Heritage Site by UNESCO, one of seven altogether in the Kathmandu Valley, which has the distinction of having the largest concentration of World Heritage Sites to be found in the world.

Leave by the west door of this extraordinary and important place. Now descend down a well-worn path and head for the Manohara River through which you may find you have to wade unless you can find a makeshift bridge to cross. Negotiate the paddy fields to where your car will be waiting beside a cluster of houses and a little tea shop.

After adjourning to your hotel to freshen up, enjoy an early evening wander, starting at the Crystal Hotel at the top of New Road and walking as straight as you can through the maze of the bazaar area. Look up to catch faces at carved windows and the lilt of an evening song.

Detour right to the **Mahabuddha Stupa** and the evening surgery of the famous ayurvedic Doctor Mana Bajracharya – ask anyone where to find his courtyard. Pass some crumbling classic *bahals*, or courtyards, and soon you reach the up-beat area of **Chetrapati** and **Thamel**, a gathering place for world travellers with lodges, trekking shops, bars and loud music. Stop for a Star beer or a Khukri rum and coke – and some fascinating people-watching – at **Tom & Jerry's**, **Rumdoodle** or at **Spam's Place**, the closest bar to an English pub in Kathmandu.

By 7.30pm or so you will be ready to emerge into **Keshar Mahal** and grab a taxi to take you to dinner at the Shangrila Hotel. On the way, notice the first floor offices of **KEEP**, **Kathmandu Environmental Education Project** (Tel: 418755 Open 10am–5pm) in the Tilicho Hotel, a trekker information centre and meeting place serving delicious cappuccino and cakes. The **Rana Keshar Library** on the corner, now housing the **Ministry of Education**, contains a nostalgic collection of unlikely books on Nepal and old hunting photographs.

The al fresco charms of the elegant **Shambala Garden Cafe** at the Shangrila Hotel are only five minutes away by cab. If it is an extremely cold night, you might prefer to dine indoors, upstairs at the **Kokonor Restaurant**.

Right, Swayambhunath stupa

Pick & Mix

These half days are deliberately designed to allow time to wander, look and absorb. If you find them too leisurely, keep moving and combine three in one day. Except where specified, these suggestions are suitable for both mornings and afternoons. The Valley is easy and safe to get around and you are encouraged to improvise and deviate from the itineraries.

1. Palaces of Patan

Explore the Durbar Square then walk to the Golden Temple, Kumbeshwar Temple and Mahabuddha.

Cycle or taxi to **Patan**, cradle of traditional arts and architecture in the Valley, which is also known by its ancient name of Lalitpur, the Beautiful City. The **Patan Durbar Square** is in the very heart of the city and must rank as one of the finest urban streetscapes in

Gilded metalwork is a feature of Patan

Golden door of Mani Keshar Chowk, Patan

the world. Visit the courtyards of the **Royal Palace**, more accessible than their Kathmandu counterparts.

The present palace structure was built in the 17th century on earlier foundations. The first courtyard, the **Sundari Chowk**, the royal living quarters, was finished in 1627. It contains the spectacular **Tusha Hiti**, the royal bathing tank with a water spout in the form of a gilded conch shell. Lined with hundreds of deities of stone and metal and in an octagonal form to emphasise the king's devotion to the eight *nagas* or serpents, the perimeter of the sunken tank is guarded by a pair of dragons carved in stone.

The entrance to the Sundari Chowk is through a very narrow doorway, to the left of a more impressive entrance which is never used as it is believed to be controlled by an evil spirit. The next courtyard, the **Mul Chowk**, was completed in 1666, and has the gilded sanctuary of the **Bidya Mandir** shrine in its centre. Another favourite house goddess of the Malla kings is enshrined in the south wing of the courtyard, guarded by life-size gilded bronze figures. The **Taleju Temple** is in the north eastern corner, and can only be entered by her priests. Note the fine doorway, a tribute to the metalworking castes for which Patan is still famous.

Next is the temple of **Degutalle**, and then the third courtyard, the **Mani Keshar Chowk**. Restored by the Austrians, it has superb exterior decoration and a lovely central gilded window from where the kings would sit to look out over their subjects and to gaze upon the magnificent **Krishna Mandir** opposite. The octagonal *shikara*-style Krishna Mandir, considered the finest stone temple in the Valley, is faced by a *garuda* on a column. Pause to enjoy the friezes depicting the epics that run clockwise around the building, rather like a cartoon strip. Adjacent to the Krishna Mandir is the **Bishwa Nath Mandir**, guarded by two huge stone elephants. It is one of the earlier temples in the square and is distinctive for its finely carved wood pillars.

Beyond is one of the most important temples, the **Bhimsen Mandir**, sacred to Bhimsen, the god of traders, and especially worshipped by the businessmen of Patan. From the centre of the top of the three-tiered roof falls a metal ribbon-like banner engraved with mantras, donated by a wealthy benefactor.

Directly opposite, the lotus-shaped **Mangal Hiti** has three stone waterspouts in the shape of crocodile heads. This Licchavi water conduit dates from the 10th century and is now well below street level. Stand back to admire the palace façades. Return to see some interesting monuments at the upper end of the Durbar Square. **Siddhi Narasinha Malla** surveys the glory he has created from the top of his stone pillar, protected by a golden *naga* or serpent. The three-tiered and arcaded **Hari Shankar Mandir** acts as a visual stop to the southern end of the square. Two-tiered **Char Narayan Mandir** was built in 1566 and the octagonal stone **Krishna Temple**, which was damaged in the 1988 earthquake, was built by a Malla princess after the deaths of both her father King Yoganarendra Malla, and her son Lokaprakasha, to gain merit for them in their next life.

Inside the 'Golden Temple' or Kwa Bahal

Leave the Durbar Square by the northwest corner, past some little shops, and find your way down the street to the right to the small entrance guarded by lions of the **Kwa Bahal** or **Golden Temple**, on your left. The most beautifully decorated of all the hundreds of two-storey Newari Buddhist monastery courtyards (for which Patan is renowned), this is an active and busy religious centre. The entire façade of the temple enshrining the Buddha is of finely executed and lavishly embellished gilded copper.

Turn left out of the Kwa Bahal and further north is the towering **Kumbheshwar Temple**. Founded in 1392, it is the oldest in

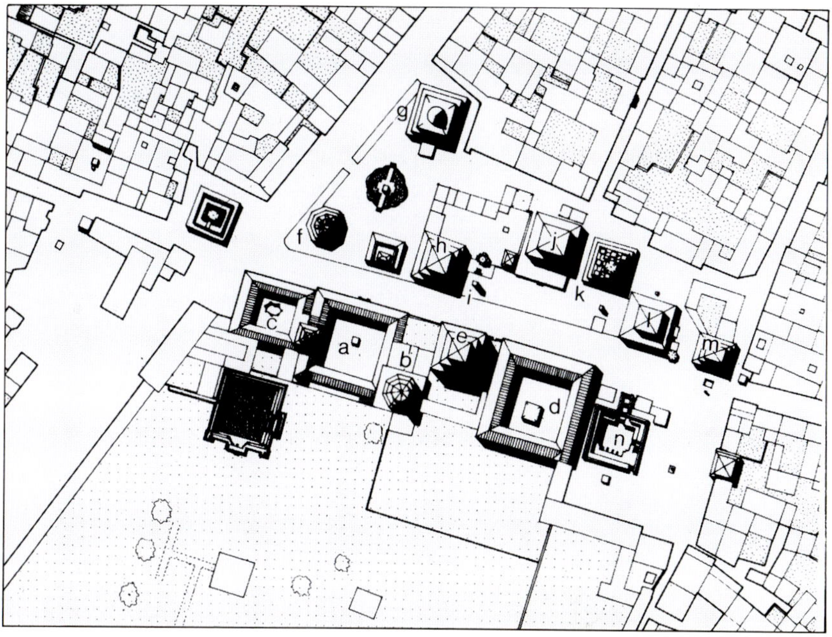

Patan Durbar Square
(a) Mul Chowk
(b) Taleju Temple
(c) Sundari Chowk
(d) Mani Keshar Chowk
(e) Degutalle
(f) Krishna Temple
(g) Bhai Dega Shiva Temple
(h) Hari Shankar
(i) Siddhi Narasinha Malla
(j) Char Narayan
(k) Krishna Mandir
(l) Bishwarnath Mandir
(m) Bhimsen Mandir
(n) Mangal Hiti

Patan and within its precincts are some early sculptures and two tanks, believed to be fed by waters from the sacred **Gosainkund Lake** high in the **Helambu** mountains. This is where the Hindu Brahmans must renew their sacred threads during the **Janai Purnima** (full moon) festival in July or August. Don't miss the **Ulmanta Bhairav** shrine south of the main temple with its fine silverwork. The northern **Ashoka stupa** is just north of here in this particularly interesting and old corner of Patan. Turning right out of the temple compound follow the road left, the stupa will be visible on the left. Cross the river and you could walk to Baneswar, enjoy the view from the top of the **Everest Hotel**, then catch a cab back.

Alternatively, return by a different route turning right to the little **Uma Maheswar**, with its beautiful 10th-century stone carving of Shiva and Parvati, recently restored by the Kathmandu Valley Preservation Trust sponsored by the British Ambassador. Passing through the Durbar Square, turn left (east), through the bustle of the vegetable market, down a narrow brick-paved street to the large terrace square containing the **Sundhara** or golden tap. Believed to have been built to refresh the **Rato Machhendra**, it is an important stopping place for his chariot. Turn right up a paved street. At the top is the narrow entrance to the remarkable terracotta **Mahabuddha**, or the Temple of the Thousand Buddhas. Badly damaged in the 1934 earthquake, the restorers were confused by the great many parts that they could not replace, so they assembled them into another shrine in the corner. Before you leave, further down the street on the left is the famous **Uku Bahal**, a renowned courtyard with gilded roofs and a wonderful collection of metal animals. This is one of the earliest *bahals*, built in the 1650s by King Shivadeva.

2. Kirtipur

The ridge city of Kirtipur was the last to fall to the forces of King Prithvi Narayan Shah when he successfully unified the Kathmandu Valley in 1769.

Bicycle or drive through the rather desultory new **Tribhuvan University** buildings and climb up to the ridge-top Newar city of **Kirtipur**. The last town to fall to the forces of King Prithvi Narayan Shah during his successful conquest of the Valley in 1768 and 1769, he was apparently so enraged by the resistance and independence of the people of Kirtipur that, when he finally overcame them, he had the noses and lips cut off all the menfolk, sparing only flute players.

Start by visiting the **Chilanchu Stupa** which surmounts the southern hill and step around the piles of grain drying on its stone flags. Once a thriving monastery, this neglected area has four smaller stupas at cardinal points around the central stupa. Wind through the narrow medieval streets, past the ladies spinning in doorways, and the children who will offer you little dolls made from remnants of the local homemade fabric industry. The clunk of the handlooms become a familiar sound as you pass the houses of Kirtipur.

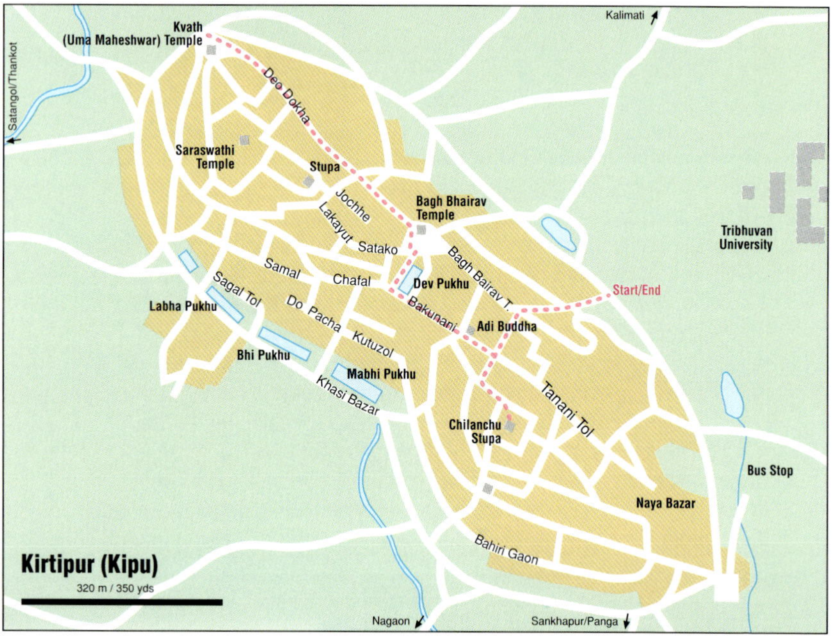

Khukris for sale

Walking west, soon you come to a tank in the middle of the town sited below the great **Bagh Bhairav Temple**, an imposing building decorated with the daggers, swords and shields captured by King Prithvi Narayan Shah; it is a place of worship for Hindus and Buddhists alike. The **Kvath** or **Uma Maheswar Temple** is at the highest point west of the town, guarded by two fine elephants atop a flight of steps. It commands a fine view across the whole Valley to the distant white Himalaya. Kirtipur has a forgotten feeling about it which makes it rather special, perhaps because of its independant history.

3. Pashupatinath and Guhyeshwari

Visit two sacred shrines that Hindus make pilgrimages to.

Pashupatinath (*see map on page 45*) is considered one of the four most important Shiva shrines in Asia and is thus the object of many pilgrimages, especially during festivals such as **Shivaratri**, when tens of thousands of devotees celebrate Shiva's birthday here in February or March. The largest temple complex in the Kathmandu Valley is so sacred that non-Hindus are forbidden to enter its courtyards. There is however still much to see, not least the cremations that are almost constantly being conducted on the banks of the Bagmati, which flows eventually into the holy Ganges. To have their feet in the sacred river at the moment of death is important for Hindus to attain instant release. Two large burning *ghats* directly beneath the main temple are reserved exclusively for the royal family. Upstream there are caves, formerly used by *sadhus* or holy men for meditation, where the river twists into a gorge above the main temple.

The temple is dedicated to Pashupati, the Lord of the Beasts, an incarnation of Shiva particularly popular in Nepal. The present structure was built in 1696 on a 15th-century site by Bupalendra Malla, after the previous building had been severely damaged by termites. Like many Valley temples, the gilded copper triple roofs are decorative, and do not have corresponding floors.

Tij festival at Pashupatinath

The best approach is from the **Bagmati Bridge** on the Ring Road, opposite the modest clubhouse of the Royal Nepal Golf Club. The golf course is on land actually owned by the temple *guthi*. Having explored the shrines and sculptures in the environs of Pashupatinath, cross the two stone bridges, climb up the long flight of steps opposite and pause on the terrace to

Shrine at Swayambhunath

look down on the complex. At the top of the hillock is the **Gorakhnath Shikhara**, and walking on through the forest down the other side, you reach **Guhyeshvari**, the counterpart to Pashupatinath, dedicated to Shiva's *shakti*, Kali. Records of this temple complex, access to which is also forbidden to non-Hindus, date from the 17th century. Enjoy the peaceful atmosphere and if you have time, explore the edge of the river.

4. Swayambhunath and Ichangu

Bijeshwari. Breakfast at the Hotel Vajra, then up to the all-seeing eyes of Swayambhunath, the oldest settlement in the Valley. Finish the morning with a walk to the village shrine of Ichangu Narayan.

If you are in a car, you might like to include a visit to the **National Museum** in **Chauni** (open 10am to 4pm, closed Tuesdays) to admire its collection of sculptures. The best direct approach to **Bijeshwari** is on foot from Kathmandu, about half an hour walk, crossing the river over the temporary **Vishnumati Bridge**. Instead of following the road left, climb the steps ahead of you to the **Bijeshwari Temple**. This Tantric shrine is especially interesting in the early morning when local people gather with their daily offerings. Stop for breakfast (or lunch) on the roof of the **Hotel Vajra**, situated just above the river, and enjoy the view of both the Swayambhunath Hill and over

the city from this remarkable hotel. Don't miss the painted ceiling in the Great Pagoda Room at the very top of the hotel.

The magnificent setting of **Swayambhunath Stupa** dominates this area as you approach it by the tarmac road. Climb the pilgrim's route up the 365 stone steps on the eastern side of the forested hill, flanked with the great animal vehicles of the five Dhyani-Buddhas (meditating buddhas) – Amogasiddhi on Garuda (north), Akshobhya on elephant (east), Patmasambhava on horse (south), Amitabha on peacock (west) and Vairocana on lion (near Akshobhya). The Dhyani-Buddhas represent different qualities attached to a Boddhisattva (Enlightened One).

Between the Buddhas we find four Buddhashakis which represent the female qualities. All around the Stupa you see prayer mills with the prayer inscription '*Om mani padme hum*'. Spinning around the prayer mill (always clockwise like the surrounding stupa) saves the believers saying the prayer. Bunches of monkeys in the whole area gave the Stupa its nickname Monkey Temple. Make sure you don't hold any sort of food in your hands while strolling around here, as the monkeys are known for becoming quite aggressive in order to snatch some food. A huge gilded copper *vajra* (tibetan: *dorje*), or thunderbolt, a symbol of absolute power, awaits you at the top.

The all-seeing eyes of supreme Buddhahood gaze from beneath the great gilded pinnacle with its 13 rings and crowning parasol. The nose, which looks rather like an incomplete question mark, is the Nepalese number 'one', *ek*, a symbol of unity.

The Stupa is also surrounded by a great number of buildings, shrines and a little Tibetan monastery which you are most welcome to visit. Four of the shrines are dedicated to the four elements: earth, water, fire and air. Another one on the northeast side of the Stupa is dedicated to Hariti (also known as Ajima), the goddess of pocks. Mothers would come here with their children to let the goddess immunize them against pocks and other diseases.

On the northern end we find a rather inconspicuous building with a very interesting story behind, called Shantipur Building. After King Gunakamadeva made the gods angry due to inbreeding a terrible drought and a famine following came over the land. With the help of a wise man called Shantikar, who lived in the building, the king tried to calm down the elements. Shantikar succeeded in gaining rule over nine *nags* (gods of snakes). He made them pay homage to the King and out of their own blood they built their images – afterwards rain was supposed to fall. Even nowadays it is said that the King of Nepal comes to the temple once in a while praising the nine snake gods.

Mingle with monks, devout Nepalis and Tibetan pilgrims prostrating themselves full-length in reverence around the stupa that is the ancient lotus island of Manjushri's Valley lake. There is little doubt that this site was established more than 2,500 years ago. Having browsed among the shrines, sculptures and monasteries, avoided the monkeys and admired the incomparable view of the

Valley, leave by the west side of the hill, picking up the car at the parking place by the monastery half way up.

Head on down the hill and through the village to the Ring Road, here bordered by a wall of prayer wheels and street sellers, and strung across with fluttering prayer flags. Cross the highway and take the dirt road west, past the bus station. The car, if you have one, must wait where the road peters out at a little shrine on a steep saddle. From here it is a half- hour walk through rice and mustard fields and past bamboo stands, cacti and stone quarries to **Ichangu Narayan**, a temple on the south side of **Nagarjun Hill**.

The two-storey temple was founded, according to legend, by King Hari Datta in the 6th century but the present building is 18th century. It is one of the four important Narayan shrines that, after a period of fasting, must be visited in one day in the **Haribodhini Ekadasi** in October or November when Vishu is welcomed back from his long summer sleep. The other three are Bishankhu Narayan, Changu Narayan and Sekh Narayan.

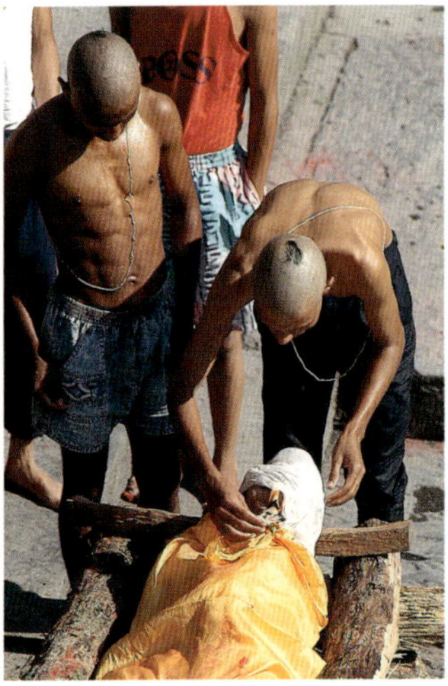

Hindu cremation

5. Bagmati Ghats

Explore the Bagmati ghats and temples of Pachali Bhairav, Tindeval, Tripura Sundari and Hem Narayan (Kalamochan). Easily reached, this seldom-visited area reveals an intimate glimpse of daily life right.

Start walking from **Tripureswar** at the small shrine of **Nav Durga** opposite the modest little Valley View Hotel. From here a dirt road leads to the holy **Bagmati River** and to the temple of the **Pachali Bhairav**, nestled in a tabernacle within the roots of a *pipal* tree. This shrine, to one of the most venerated forms of Shiva, is guarded by the sleeping **Baital**, who is worshipped on Tuesday and Saturday evenings and adorned with flowers, rice and smeared with vermilion powder.

Walk on to the river, past the crumbling **Laxmeswar Shrine** on the right, where most of the courtyard has gone and much of the woodcarving is going. The charm of this area lies in its living decay. Across the footbridge are the mineral springs of the **Rajghat**.

Turn left along the Bagmati *ghats* where Hindus traditionally burn their dead, though today a cremation is more likely to be further west at **Tekuo** at the confluence of the Vishnumati with the Bagmati rivers. Behind the *chaityas* and statues is the interesting temple complex of **Tindeval**, a fine example of the Indian *shikhara* style. Nepal's religious harmony is visible in Shiva's trident standing next to Buddhist symbols of enlightenment. Walk 10 minutes down the path along the river bank, past the pottery that makes decorative balustrades, and past the brick and stucco police barracks, until the roofs of the **Tripura Sundari** can be seen set back to the left within a fine courtyard. Built in 1818 by Queen Tripurasundari, the temple stands on a broad base with small temples at each corner and roof struts depicting stories from the *Mahabharata* epic.

The splendid white dome of the **Hem Narayan** or **Kalamochan**, guarded by rampant golden lions at each corner, is a little further on past a handsome red-smeared Hanuman, the monkey god, and across a small stream. This temple of obvious Moghul influence was built in 1852 by Jung Bahadur Rana to celebrate victories at war. It has a very fine statue of him set on a stone pillar and good woodcarvings. Leave the Hem Narayan by the opposite gate from the river and you are back in Tripureswar, close to **Patan Bridge**.

6. The Great Ashoka Stupas

Visit the four historically evocative stupas (the fifth central one is lost) which, if indeed erected in the 3rd century BC by Emperor Ashoka, the Mauryan king of northern India, make Patan the oldest Buddhist city in the world.

You will need a car or taxi for this unusual circuit of ancient stupas, which are neither equidistant from the centre of Patan nor occupy cardinal points of the compass. However they are immensely evocative with their origins shrouded in legend. Except for the eastern one which is plastered and whitewashed, the typical shallow domes of the stupas remain grass-covered.

Life on the street: a Tamang woman washes her reluctant son

Start with the northern **Epi Stupa** behind the **Kumbeshwar Temple** to which it is best to walk from the Patan Durbar Square (see Itinerary 1, *Pick & Mix*). Returning to the Durbar Square, drive east through the winding narrow streets of the eastern outskirts of Patan to the Ring Road. Straight across, the eastern **Teta Stupa** (my favourite) stands forgotten amidst fields on the left of the little-used road to **Lubhu**.

Follow the Ring Road south; instead of taking the route left at the crossroads to **Godavari**, turn right. After a short distance is the southern **Lagan Stupa**. The top is supposed to be the only point in the Valley from where you can see Mount Everest. Go on down the road. You pass on the right the extensive buildings of the Patan Hospital and on your leftthe outskirts of Patan.

To reach the fourth western stupa, turn right at the zoo roundabout at **Jawalakhel**; look out for the Hotel Narayani as you go down the hill and the **Pulchok Stupa** is opposite on the left. Explore behind it and climb to the restored **Akshyashore Mahavihar** on an early Licchavi site.

7. Follow the Rato Machhendra

Breakfast or lunch at the Himalaya Hotel, then visit Patan, Jawalakhel and the 16th-century country villages of Khokana and Bungamati, winter home of the Rato Machhendra.

Enjoy the view and the food from the **Base Camp coffee shop** or by the pool at the **Himalaya Hotel**. On foot, turn left out of the hotel and keep left through Patan Gate and into the old part of the city. Skirt the Durbar Square and head south to one of the most popular temples in Patan, the **Rato Machhendranath Temple**, dedicated to the powerful Tantric deity who guards the Valley and is worshipped as the god of rain and plenty. His beautiful temple stands in an open square and has intricately carved doorways and struts, and graceful windbells lining the metal roofs.

The **Rato Machhendra** is paraded through Patan every summer in a huge chariot culminating in the festival of **Bhoto Jatra** at **Jawalakhel**. The exact month is fixed by astrologers, and a sacred bejewelled waistcoat, or *bhoto*, supposedly belonging to the serpent king, is displayed in the presence of the royal family. The chariot is then dismantled, except once every 12 years (the next occasion is in 2003) when the chariot is dragged to the Rato Machhendra's second residence at **Bungamati**, a village 3 miles (5km) south down a steep and rugged road. This is a difficult task undertaken very seriously because, it is said, if the chariot fails to reach Bungamati within a certain time, the god will be taken to Bhaktapur.

You may wish to visit the **Patan Zoo** with its man-eating tiger brought from Chitwan. It is said that the Patan Zoo is in itself a mu-

seum of sad Victorian zoo conditions. Explore the good Tibetan carpet shops around the **Tibetan Refugee Camp** and call in to watch them being dyed and woven in the traditional manner. Handmade carpets are Nepal's biggest export industry and their production employs over 200,000 Nepalis in the Valley. Turn right at the big tree to the painting shop of the artist **B B Thapa**, who sells charming Nepal views in the primitive style of the Sherpan and Tibetan tradition.

Take a taxi or have your car meet you here and, crossing the Ring Road, take the processionary route, lined with votive *chaityas*, to the twin settlements of **Bungamati** and **Khokana**. Visit the *shikara*-style **Rato Machhendranath Temple**, where the powerful deity has spent his winter months since 1593, carried here most years from Patan in a simple palanquin except for the marathon when the huge chariot must negotiate this road. Visit the image of Bhairav in his nearby **Lokeshwar Shrine**.

From Bungamati it is a short walk to **Khokana**, but be sure to detour uphill to the important Ganesh shrine of **Karya Binayak** set in a pretty forest clearing. The single-storey temple in a walled compound is often busy with families requesting help from the accommodating elephant god, Ganesh, who specialises in completing difficult tasks.

There is a beautiful view from this peaceful rural shrine across the yellow mustard fields to the western foothills. When you reach Khokana, seek out the mustard oil presses for which this village is famous for and the **Shekali Mai** shrine, dedicated to one of the Valley's nature goddesses.

8. Manjushri's Gorge and Kali's Sacrifice

Excursion to Chobar, Pharping and Dakshinkali, by car or bicycle, visiting the temples in this historic corner of the Valley.

If you are planning to bicycle, take a packed lunch as Dakshinkali, the furthest point, is 14 miles (22km) from Kathmandu.

Stop first at **Chobar** (see IFC-1 map) where, legend tells us, the god Manjushri released the Valley lake by smiting a gorge with his sword. The Bagmati River indeed drains the Valley through a narrow gorge which slices through the Chobar Hill, though today this natural wonder is much disfigured by a belching cement factory. It is hard to ignore the results of its pollution as you climb up the steps to the **Adinath Temple**, a triple-roofed Buddhist temple built in 1640 and decorated with numerous household implements; water vessels, cooking pots and pans. A metal suspension bridge spans the gorge, imported from Scotland in 1903.

Just south is the riverside shrine of **Jal Binayak**, honouring a massive rock **Ganesh**, where people who seek strength of character, worship. Also enshrined here is the thunderbolt said to have been hurled at the Valley wall by Krishna in the alternative version of the legend of the lake. The road south passes the small **Taudaha Lake**, created by Manjushri, according to legend, to house the *nagas* (serpents) stranded when the Valley was drained.

Follow the twists and turns of the river, with the bulk of **Champa Devi Hill** (7,477ft/2,279m) looming on the right and take a detour for breakfast or lunch to the **Himalayan Heights Resort** (Tel: 290-622) at **Hatiban**. The turning to the right is marked on the telephone pole and the road climbs steeply for 15 minutes to this pleas-

Chobar Gorge

ant stone-built hotel on a high flank overlooking the valley and white peaks. The main road eventually reaches the lovely town of **Pharping**, just outside the Valley at an altitude of 5,148ft (1,570m). The rock temple of **Shekh Narayan Temple** honours Vishnu and stands above a series of pools full of fish, a place of pilgrimage since the 15th century. Further up the same hill is the thriving Tibetan Buddhist monastery and meditation centre at the **Goraknath Cave**, sacred to the Tibetan saint, Guru Padma Sambhava, whose footprints, carved on the platform, are dated 1390. Above Pharping is the 17th-century temple of **Vajra Yogini Temple**, not be confused with the Sankhu temple of the same name. The Tantric goddess' pleasant visage belies her awesome instruments, a chopper with a *vajra* handle and skull cap.

Pilgrim at Dakshinkali

Several miles below Pharping is the shrine of **Dakshinkali**, or southern Kali, at the bottom of a flight of stairs in a dark natural recess at a confluence between two forested hillsides. The goddess's insatiable appetite is appeased by twice-weekly sacrifices, Saturday and Tuesday, when the blood of male goats and chickens bathe the black stone image of Kali, the consort of Shiva in her most terrible form. The headless carcases are transformed into picnics for the faithful on the slopes above this sinister spot. The simpler shrine of Kali's mother is up a hill beyond the lower temple.

9. Bishankhu Narayan

Walk from the Godavari road to the temple of Bishankhu Narayan. Beware, as only those pure of sin can fit through a narrow cleft in the rock. Visit the Royal Botanical Gardens at Godavari.

Leave early in the morning to enjoy the view of the mountains, the activity in the fields and the village life through which you pass. Carry a packed meal to avoid going back early for lunch.

Taking the radial to **Godavari** from the Ring Road, pass through the villages of **Harisiddhi Bhawani Temple** and **Thaiba**, reminiscent of a Bruegel masterpiece in their symphony of colors and textures. At the end of the next town, **Baregaon**, take the dirt road northeast. Leave the car at the first village road to await your return and enjoy walking through this magical corner of the Valley.

The road climbs to a saddle from which, on a clear morning, you can see as far west at the white peaks of the **Annapurna** range, north of Pokhara. The temple of **Bishankhu Narayan** is little more than a natural cave at the top of a steep stairway, but it is one of the most celebrated Vishnu shrines in the Valley. According to legend, Shiva once hid here from the demon, Bhasmasur, who had the power to turn all living things into dust and ashes at his touch. Vishnu convinced the demon to touch his own forehead and the demon turned himself to dust; the hillock adjacent to the cave is said to be made of the ashes of Bhasmasur.

After returning to the car, drive on to the village of **Godavari** where the marble quarry scars a hillside on the right. Above you is the highest hill on the rim of the Valley, **Phulchoki** (9,062ft/2,762m), which is a lovely place for early morning birdwatching and spring walks in the rhododendron forests.

The first boarding school in Nepal was opened in Godavari in 1951 by American Jesuits, who still run one of the finest schools in the Valley. Founded by the late Father Moran – the ham radio enthusiast who was one of the first foreigners to be granted Nepali citizenship – the school welcomes interested educators as visitors.

Pass beneath the tall trees and you will see the stone buildings of the school set back on your right. Follow the road down the hill to the **Royal Botanical Gardens**, well worth a visit and a good place to linger, except on Saturday when its peace is shattered by the mandatory stereos that accompany every party of picnickers.

10. Everest Flight to Enchantment

The Mountain Flight along the Himalaya to Mount Everest.

Every morning one of Nepal's airlines flies east from Kathmandu for one hour along the snow white peaks of the Himalaya to view **Mount Everest** (29,028ft/8,848m). The highest mountain in the

Mount Everest

Kangchenjunga from the air

world sits bestride the Nepal-Tibet border, and is known as Sagarmatha (Mother of the Universe) in Nepal and as Chomolungma (Mother Goddess of the Snow) in Tibet. You are normally invited to photograph, or simply to marvel, from the cockpit. Lifting even the most jaded of spirits, this flight to enchantment is an opportunity to enjoy the subtle colours of the intricate cobweb of terraced hillsides of the Mahabharat, or middle hills, as well as to glory in the awesome heights and ranges of the highest chain of mountains in the world.

To join the flight, book early (tel: 220-757) and hope for crystal clear weather.

Nepal, Top Of The World

A mecca for mountaineers, climbers and trekkers, Nepal has eight of the 10 highest mountains in the world and eight of the world's fourteen 26,250ft (8,000m) peaks within or on its borders. They are:

1. **Everest** (Sagarmatha, Chomolungma) in the Himalaya range on Nepal-Tibet (China) border — 29,028ft/ 8,848m
2. **K-2** (Chogari; sometimes called Mt. Goodwin Austin, but this name is not officially recognised) in the Karakorum range on the Pakistan-China border — 28,251ft/ 8,611m
3. **Kangchenjunga** Himalaya, Nepal-India border — 28,169ft/ 8,586m
4. **Lhotse** Himalaya, Nepal-Tibet border — 27,940ft/ 8,516m
5. **Makalu** Himalaya, Nepal-Tibet border — 27,766ft/ 8,463m
6. **Cho Oyu** Himalaya, Nepal-Tibet border — 26,906ft/ 8,201m
7. **Dhaulagiri 1** Himalaya, Nepal — 26,795ft/ 8,167m
8. **Manaslu** Himalaya, Nepal — 26,781ft/ 8,163m
9. **Nanga Parbat** Hindu Kush, Pakistan — 26,657ft/ 8,125m
10. **Annapurna 1** Himalaya, Nepal — 26,545ft/ 8,091m
11. **Gasherbrum 1** Karakoram, Pakistan (Hidden Peak) — 26,470ft/ 8,068m
12. **Broad Peak** Karakoram, Pakistan — 26,401ft/ 8,047m
13. **Shisha Pangma** (Xixabangma, Gosainthan) Himalaya, Tibet (China) — 26,398ft/ 8,046m
14. **Gasherbrum 11** Karakoram, Pakistan — 26,362ft/ 8,035m

Day Trips

11. Sankhu Goddess and Gokarna Golf Course

Explore the old trading town of Sankhu and the shrine of the Bajra Jogini. Return for lunch and in the afternoon, enjoy the facilities at the Gokarna Safari Park.

Arrange a car for the day or bicycle the 12 miles (19km) to the sleepy town of **Sankhu** (see IFC-1 map), in the northeast part of the Valley, a historical stop on the old trading route to Tibet. After investigating the town, follow the road that continues only a little way north beyond the town and becomes a wide path, paved with stone. The important temple to the mysterious goddess **Bajra Jogini** is a climb up a steep flight of steps hidden among tall dark pines. She is portrayed in a fine gold *torana* above the door of the three-roofed structure; notice the roof struts with figures of various deities. The neighbouring **Gunivihar Temple** has an interesting *chaitya*. There are other shrines and sculptures in the **Vajra Yogini Dyochhen**, further up the hill. Legend has the Tantric goddess residing here from primeval history, and she is credited with having persuaded Manjushri to drain the Valley lake.

Spotted deer or chital

Rejoin your car in Sankhu and return down the road for lunch in the restaurant just in front of the entrance at **Gokarna Safari Park**, also known as the **King's Forest**. You will have to park the car outside unless you are playing golf, and pay a nominal entry fee. Spend the afternoon in this pleasant setting. (It is best avoided on weekends when it becomes crowded with diplomat golfers and local picnickers.)

You can choose from a pretty but tricky nine-hole golf course, rent a horse for riding, or explore the forest on foot or from the back of an elephant. It is a pleasant trot in their pony and trap, but watch you don't get hit on the head by a golf ball. You are very likely to see almost-tame *chital* (spotted deer) and black buck wandering on the fringes of the forest and there is a huge python in a cage. Bird watching is good in the forest here, especially if you linger until late afternoon or stop off in the early morning.

Do a round of prayer wheels at **Bodhnath**, which you will pass on the way back. Remember, it is most auspicious to circumambulate an odd-number of times, and always clockwise, keeping the stupa on your right.

12. Tantric Temple and Shiva Screen at Lele

A bicycle ride (or arrange a car for the day) through the southern Valley towns of Sunakothi, Thecho, Chapagaon and Lele visiting the temples of Vajra Varahi and Tika Bhairav.

Turn off the Ring Road and head south at the turning marked with a red sign to the Leprosy Hospital at Anandaban, just west of the Godavari turning – be careful as some local maps are misleading. This will be an enchanting rural day in a little-known corner of the Valley. You will enjoy the terraced green rice fields, scarlet poinsettias and spikey brown cactus in the hedgerows, with always the chance of wide views of the white mountains behind.

The road passes through the 16th-century town of **Sunakothi** (see IFC-1 map)but you might be tempted to stop a while in the next, more friendly, settlement of **Thecho**. The **Balkumari Temple** overlooks a square used for drying golden grain and red chillies, and plenty of noisy clamouring children.

A mile (1.6km) on is the pleasant old town of **Chapagaon**, where the surfaced road deteriorates to dirt. There are some erotic carvings on the **Bhairav Shrine** in the village. Follow the path east out of the town to the important Tantric site of the **Vajra Varahi Temple**, in a grove of sacred trees. Naturally shaped stones are

Chapagaon from the Lele road

worshipped here as images of Ganesh, Bhairav and the Ashta Matrikas and on the edge of the trees are some old cremation grounds.

Returning to the main road south, there is a particularly good place to eat your picnic lunch, with fine views and shady trees, if you can find it. The spot is tucked high above the left side of the road on a corner just before it drops down into the **Lele Valley**. Visit the eye-opening **Leprosy Hospital** in the village of **Anandaban**, which is well marked with red and white signs.

If you have the energy to continue on down the deteriorating road, be sure to look for the **Tika Bhairav** shrine to the right of the road on the edge of the village of **Lele**. It is not a temple in any conv-entional sense. Look for a huge brick wall, 10 by 20ft (2 by 6m) painted with a wonderful, monumental abstract close-up of Bhairav, Shiva in his most terrible form. Lele is just beyond the edge of the Valley and the drive to this remote corner is well rewarded with unspoiled countryside and clean fresh air.

13. Sleeping Vishnus and Kakani Emissaries

Balaju Vishnu and the 22 Water Spouts. Drive to Kakani. Walk to Budhanilkantha and see the sleeping Vishnu before returning.

Arrange a car and driver for the day and start by visiting the Licchavi **Balaju Reclining Vishnu** and the **22 Water Spouts**, the largest *hiti* in the Valley and always busy with people washing and bathing. These are located (see IFC-1 map) in the small park on the left in the town of **Balaju** just across the Ring Road northwest of Kathmandu. At the foot of the forested **Nagarjun hill**, a favourite place for bird watchers and picnickers, this is a special little corner, very popular with locals. Try and avoid the public swimming pool.

Drive on past the main entrance to the Nagarjun forest and wind up the Trisuli road for about one hour (18 miles/29km) through the terraces and bamboo stands. At the very top, turn sharp right to **Kakani**, a small village perched high on the rim of the Valley.

Kakani has a large police training school and a wonderful view. Enjoy it from the garden of the **Taragaon Hotel** and peek over the barbed-wire fence at the original Raj-style bungalow that has belonged to successive British emissaries since 1850.

At that time the British Resident's movements were greatly restricted, even within the Valley which he was forbidden to leave, and this property was given by Jung Bahadur Rana himself as their own private retreat. Carried up by servants or arriving on ponies with their own personal army bodyguards, here the first foreign residents of Nepal could relax uninhibited by the restrictions and formalities of 19th-century court life. They were free to play golf or hunt for barking deer, *chukor* partridge or pheasant, signalling when in need of further supplies to their Kathmandu Residence by heliograph, a complicated system of flashing mirrors which relied on line of sight.

Reclining Vishnu at Budhanilkantha

Leave the car, and be sure the driver knows you wish to be met beside the great Vishnu at Budhanilkantha. Set off northeast along the line of the ridge towards the fruit farm, then seek local advice to find the trail that bears east around the flanks of the **Shivapuri Hills** – the highest peak is 8,940ft (2,732m).

Resist the temptation to go down to your right or you will end up back in Balaju. It can be warm on this south-facing hill so be sure you carry adequate drinking water. Follow the trail for about four hours, picnicking on the way, and enjoy the wonderful view south over the entire Kathmandu Valley.

Eventually you will reach the village of **Budhanilkantha** which is close to the vanished Licchavi town called Thatungri Dranga. Pass the brick-built compound of the British-subsidized secondary school, where the Crown Prince was a former pupil, and visit the ancient **Reclining Vishnu**.

The largest and most powerful of the four Vishnus in the Valley, this massive Licchavi sculpture is made from a massive black stone that must have been dragged from far beyond the Valley. Lying on a bed of huge coiled *nagas* or serpents, a forecast of death forbids the kings of Nepal, themselves incarnations of Vishnu, from looking at the monumental image. Recent renovations have sadly felled the *pipal* tree which shaded the image and imprisoned it behind concrete bars. From here it is a only a 6-mile (9-km) drive south to Kathmandu.

14. Dhulikhel to Panauti

Long day hike from Dhulikhel, via Namo Buddha, to Panauti.

This is a good five-hour walk and nearly two hours' drive in total, so leave Kathmandu latest by 8.30am after a good breakfast. Carry a daypack with a waterbottle and a packed lunch. You will need a car to drop you at **Dhulikhel** (see IFC-1 map). Ask the driver to pick you up at about 3pm from Panauti and ask him to wait by the Brahmayana Temple at the confluence of the rivers.

Turn right into the town of Dhulikhel, then left past the new buildings and government offices in this regional headquarters. Start walking up a wide well-worn trail and soon the climb reaches a little shrine and you are rewarded by spectacular mountain views extending as far west as the **Annapurnas** and even **Dhaulagiri** on a good day. Asking people as you go and skirting the jeep track, it will take you about three hours to reach the gleaming white stupa of **Namo Buddha** on the **Namara hill**. It is a lovely, varied walk through fields and forests with constantly delightful views and, at one point, a rather alarming landslide.

Explore the prayer-flag-bedecked stupa, small monastery and newly-donated *mani* wall. Important to Tibetan Buddhists, this sacred spot is where, according to legend, the Lord Buddha offered himself to a starving tigress and her cubs.

Eat lunch with a 360° view on the very highest point before dropping down on the western side of the hill to **Namara**, with its Swayambhunath-like stupa and huge prayer-wheel. The trail descends steeply through sacred forests, then meanders through villages and cultivated fields along a pretty valley. Take note of some remarkable Ganesh shrines and fine woodcarvings on the *dharmasalas*, or travellers' resthouses, in the villages on this pilgrims' route. This is the most impressive approach to **Panauti**, and the artistic jumble of temple roofs clustered at the **Pungamati Confluence** gleam in the sun. Be sure to find the energy to explore this fascinating town (*see Day 2 itinerary*) with its very early and precious temples.

Right, pilgrim route to Namo Buddha

EXCURSIONS

Despite the density of the richness of Kathmandu Valley, the real wealth of Nepal can only be appreciated by a visit to the mountains, rivers and jungles beyond the Valley. Nepal is compact, so the diversity intrinsic in this beautiful country can be enjoyed in a series of well-planned overnight visits.

Nepal is criss-crossed with trails and trade routes, making it ideal for trekking trips of four days to four weeks or more. Trekking requires not only time, but an enjoyment of camping and walking, as there are inevitable ups and downs in the Himalayan terrain, and flat ridge walking is relatively rare. With a reputable agent, trekking is a luxurious experience compared with the Westerner's concept of backpacking. Not only are there porters to carry all but a light daypack, but tents are erected, tables and stools provided and meals cooked by an unfailingly cheerful team of Sherpa guides.

Nepal's road network is less comprehensive, so without the time or desire to trek, these suggestions are necessarily restricted to driving and flying. The routes that follow will give you a feel of Nepal. Combine them as you please; link them into a longer trip, or choose one if your time is short.

The rhododendron, with Machhapuchhre's distinctive Fishtail peak

15. Trisuli River

Drive early down the Pokhara road to the Trisuli River. Spend the day river running in rubber rafts, riding the rapids and enjoying the scenery at the leisurely speed of the river. Camp overnight on a white-sand beach. Next day, continue down river, then drive back to Kathmandu.

Several huge river systems drain the Himalaya, tumbling from the heights of Tibet fed by milky glaciers, racing past the terraces of the middle hills until they slow down, through the **Terai** lowlands and meandering eventually into the Ganges. The middle stretches of these rivers with evocative names such as the **Bheri**, the **Karnali**, the **Kali Gandaki**, the **Seti**, the **Sun Koshi**, the **Dudh Kosi** and the **Arun** can take days and even weeks to run.

With the advantage of both convenience and accessibility, a two-day trip on the **Trisuli River** offers a lovely opportunity to experience the joys of rural Nepal at the relaxed pace of the river. Choose a reliable operator, and they will make all the arrangements at a fixed cost. This will include securing a river permit, arranging the car, providing the boat and a trained crew, all meals and all camping equipment. I recommend **Himalayan River Exploration** (PO Box 170, Naxal, Kathmandu. Tel: 418-491; Telex: 2216; Fax: 414-075), who pioneered the industry of river edge over running in Nepal, maintain stringent safety standards and offer the best facilities.

The road climbs out of the early-morning Valley past the town of **Thankot**, the earth-satellite station and King Tribhuvan's polite wave. With clear skies, the first glimpse of **Himalchuli** (25,896ft/7,893m) and **Manaslu** (26,781ft/8,163m), will take your breath away as you reach the rim. The main road to India drops down to the truck-stop village of **Naubise**, where it divides. Branch right and on through the hills until you get to the put-in point at the village of **Kuringhat**, where you bump down to the river edge over sculptured stones and crashing waters. The rubber boats are supported by a rowing frame and piloted by an experienced oarsman. Your personal belongings are stowed in black waterproof bags and sealed ammunition boxes. Although always within reach of the road, the river trip travels self-sufficient of camping gear, food, drink and helpers to assist in both rowing and camping, as well as interpreting the sights and sounds of the riverside villages and the flora and fauna of the riverbanks.

Pausing at a wayside shrine, exploring a simple settlement or waving at curious children, a day on the river is hard to beat. Between the adrenalin rush of the rapids, all with alluring names and some of which change with the seasons, the flat, calm stretches provide ample opportunity for swimming, relaxing and simply reflecting. Sleep in tents on the sand beaches after an evening around a driftwood fire.

The river trip ends early afternoon of the second day, when the imposing bridge at the roadside town of **Mugling** comes into view. Here the road divides to **Pokhara** (a three-hour drive) or to **Narayanghat** (one hour). It is about three hours' drive back to Kathmandu. If there is time, another day floating on the river brings you to the **Royal Chitwan National Park** (*see Itinerary 17, Excursions*).

Machhapuchhre and the Annapurnas reflected in Phewa Lake, Pokhara

16. Pokhara: Magnificent Mountains

The verdant Pokhara valley is 124 miles (200km) west of Kathmandu. The old trading bazaar of Pokhara, beneath the towering Annapurna Himal, is dominated by the distinctive peak of Machhapuchhre, the sacred Fishtail. Stay for one or two nights by the lakeside to enjoy the sleepy atmosphere and the stunning views.

Take a half-hour flight from Kathmandu west to **Pokhara** along the mountains, sitting on the right side of the aircraft for the best view. Driving takes six hours, and longer if you detour to the restored 15th-century palace and temple of **Gorkha**, seat of King Prithvi Narayan Shah, who united Nepal in 1768 and founded the present dynasty. Ideally, drive there from Kathmandu, and fly back.

Set in the wide, lush, green valley of the **Seti River**, the old trading town of Pokhara sprawls over several miles. Decorated pony trains from the Kali Gandaki trade routes jostle with men from the mountains bartering in the bazaar. Buses hoot and trekkers stride down the street *en route* for the hills.

More peaceful is the **Phewa Lake**, south of the airstrip and the main town. On a clear morning the snowy outlines of the **Annapurna Himal** and the unmistakable **Fishtail** peak of **Machhapuchhre** are reflected in its depths. Here, enjoy the restful atmosphere of this almost tropical valley of Nepal. Jacaranda, banana and papaya trees flourish at this altitude of about 3,000ft (900m).

If you want to do more than relax, there are day walks to **Sarangkot** and **Naudanda**, or much more interesting is to walk up towards **Kalikathan** on the first day of the Royal Trek or explore the pretty valley beyond **Lake Begnas**, east of Pokhara. Tourists visit the **Mahendra Caves** and the **Hyangja Tibetan Village** but more fun is the **Tibetan Camp** at **Pardi** and **Devi's Fall** (also Patale Chhango), where the river disappears underground into a sinister hole. Keen birders should visit the fascinating **Pheasant Farm**, (strictly by appointment only. Tel: 061-20039), belonging to the legendary Colonel Jimmy Roberts, 'father of trekking'. Donations are welcome for the World Pheasant Association projects in Nepal.

Depending on your budget and mood, choose to stay in the **Fishtail**

Lodge (Tel: 061-20071 but book well in advance. PO Box 140, Kathmandu. Tel: 221-711; Telex: 2205; Fax: 225-236), which has an unrivalled position by the lake.

Better value is the **Hotel Mount Annapurna** (Tel: 061-20027/20037) across from the airport with good roof-top views. This modest Tibetan managed hotel has fun murals. Also recommended is the scrupulously clean **Gurkha Lodge**, run by an ex-officer and his British wife, Shirley, behind the lake opposite the Fishtail Lodge. There are only four lovely rooms set in a secluded garden.

17. Chitwan Jungle Jaunt

In one of the most beautiful wildlife areas in Asia, Tiger Tops has been operating memorable trips to this former hunting reserve well before it became Royal Chitwan National Park. Choose from a combination of nights at the world-famous Tiger Tops Jungle Lodge, the Tented Camp for wildlife devotees or the Tharu Safari Resort for a unique mix of comfort and village life on the edge of the jungle.

It is a half hour's flight every day in a Twin Otter aircraft to Tiger Tops' **Meghauli** grass airstrip, where you are met and escorted by landrover or elephant across the **Buri Rapti River** and into **Royal Chitwan National Park** (350 sq miles/900 sq km). This airstrip was extended at the visit of Queen Elizabeth II in 1961, for what was to be one of the last of the great tiger hunts in this historic region, where royalty and viceroys had been hosted for decades by the rulers of Nepal. Tiger Tops can also be reached by a five-hour drive from Kathmandu or Pokhara, or a three-day trip down the river.

The survival of the **Terai** wildlife of Nepal was threatened when the endemic malaria was eradicated in the 1950s, and large numbers of hill people settled in the Chitwan valley, clearing the forest habitat for cultivation. Chitwan is at an altitude of 450ft (140m). The fear of an unknown Nepal, and malaria fever had effectively acted as a southern blockade, deterring potential invaders and isolating the few indigenous Tharu people who had developed a partial resistance to the disease.

Tiger Tops safari tents

Gazetted in 1972, this park was first set aside to protect not the

Viewing Greater One-horned rhinoceros

magnificent **Royal Bengal tiger**, but the **Greater One-horned rhinoceros** whose prehistoric bulk, with its characteristic folds of skin, thrives in the tall grassland areas of the lowland **Terai**. Once hunted for its lucrative horn valued by the Chinese for medicinal properties, poaching is now virtually unknown.

Another important endangered species found in the Narayani River is the **Gharial crocodile**, with its long narrow snout developed for catching fish. The wildlife of Chitwan is rich and diverse, with over 450 species of birds, including all the summer migrants and winter visitors.

The elephant grass grows to 25ft (8m) in height and makes the domestic elephant an essential and practical means of conveyance. Some species of the mixed riverine forest include the *bombax*, or silk cotton tree, with its red blossom and later, white cotton which showers the forest floor, and the brilliant orange flame-of-the-forest. The tall *sal* trees (*Shorea robusta*), with their large, flat leaves grow on higher ground in the **Siwalik (Churia) Range**, the last wave of the Himalaya along the Indian border. This part of the park is home to the elusive **gaur**, the world's largest wild cattle.

Tiger Tops (PO Box 242, Kathmandu. Tel: 222-706, 415-659: Fax: 414-075 and 419-126) will show you the glories of Chitwan, from the elegant tree-top rooms of **Tiger Tops Jungle Lodge** in the heart of the park, or from the comfort of the **Tented Camp** on a plateau commanding views across the whole width of Nepal. There are knowledgeable naturalists guide walks and landrover-drives through the forest, visits to *machans* (hides) over-

Machans, or blinds, for wildlife viewing

looking *tals* (small lakes) and boat trips down the Rapti and Narayani rivers. The best part is to ride the elephants in search of wild animals, or to bathe with them in the river at the elephant camp.

First opened in 1964, Tiger Tops pioneered controlled eco-sensitive tourism with its solar energy, wildlife research programmes and educational services for the local communities.

The **Tiger Tops Tharu Safari Resort**, set in a beautiful wild garden on the edge of the park, offers a combination of more general wildlife and cultural activities and is open all the year round. The spacious rooms are styled after Tharu longhouses, decorated with artefacts and mud paintings; there is a swimming pool, nightly local dancing and a stable of horses and ponies on which to explore the surrounding countryside and villages.

18. Karnali Wildlife Wonders

Royal Bardia National Park, in far west Nepal, is the favoured destination for the true wilderness enthusiast, rich in all the wildlife of the subcontinent. The two-hour drive from Nepalganj to Tiger Tops Karnali Lodge and Tented Camp is through virgin forest and attractive Tharu villages.

Providing you have at least three nights and a real interest in wild places, it is worth making the extra effort required to get to **Royal Bardia National Park**, reached by air via the Terai town of **Nepalganj** in the far west. Due to its easy accessibility, Chitwan is in danger of overcrowding, whereas the 374 sq miles (968 sq km) of Bardia remains untouched.

Sunset on the Karnali River

Karnali Tented Camp

The main attraction is the variety of bird and animal life, including the wild elephant, swamp deer, blue bull and ghoral that do not occur in Chitwan. Baiting is still permitted in Bardia, making it one of the best places to see the **Royal Bengal tiger**. Also found are the **leopard**, **rhinoceros**, **sambar**, **chital**, **wild boar**, **Rhesus** and **Langur monkeys**, **Gharial** and **Marsh Mugger crocodiles** and **Gangetic dolphins**.

This part of the western Terai is the home of the most colourful group of **Tharu**, the collective name given to the original animistic people who farm, hunt and fish in the *dun* (valleys) of Nepal's lowlands. Adorned with magnificent silver jewellery, brilliantly coloured skirts and navy-tattooed ankles, the proud women of the Dangaura Tharu live in unique longhouses. Accommodating as many as 30 families and their livestock, these intriguing mud buildings shelter under huge grass roofs and owe little to the modern world. Divided into rooms by large moulded vats of grain, the inhabitants' belongings hang in baskets from the roof.

Explore the forests and *phantas* (short grasslands) of this beautiful national park by elephant, jeep and on foot, and travel by boat on the massive **Karnali River**, which spills out through its narrow gorge onto the plains of the Terai. One of the great wilderness experiences for the intrepid traveller is the four-day white-water trip down the **Bheri River**. Fishing for **mahseer**, the mighty sport fish of the Himalaya, is at its best in February and March when the snow-fed waters are clear. Photographed and weighed, the catch is then released to fight another day.

All arrangements are made by Tiger Tops (PO Box 242, Kathmandu. Tel: 222-706, 415-659; Telex: 2216; Fax: 414-075), who will book the 45-minute flight to Nepalganj where you are met and escorted on the two-hour drive through the villages and jungles to Bardia. **Tiger Tops Karnali Lodge**, with its timber and thatch roofs, terraces and 12 comfortable rooms, is on the edge of the park, adjacent to the Tharu villages. The **Karnali Tented Camp** stretches along the banks of the Karnali River, tucked away within the forest and evoking days of the Raj with its safari tents and attentive service, all the more appreciated for being in this remote sanctuary.

Fishing for Mahseer

Sun Koshi gorge, on the road to Tibet

19. A Walk on the Wild Side of Tibet

Drive to the Tibet border town of Zhangmu (Khasa) and stay overnight in the Zhangmu Hotel. Drive up the gorge to Nyalam, through the Himalayan range and onto the Tibetan plateau. Cross two spectacular passes to Tingri for a wonderful view of the mountains, including the peaks of Everest and Cho Oyu. Return to Khasa for the night. On the following day return to Kathmandu, stopping for lunch at the Dhulikhel Mountain Resort.

It must be stressed that this is a tough trip due to the altitude and can be very difficult to operate owing to a number of circumstances. The Chinese visa regulations for Tibet are subject to change, but at the moment are only granted to a group of at least four, and require several days' stay in Kathmandu to secure; secondly, the Chinese, who do not permit vehicles to cross the border, may not be able to supply vehicles of their own; and thirdly, the road between Kathmandu and the Tibetan plateau is not infrequently blocked by either landslides (in summer) or snow (in winter). Even if all these conditions are favourable, the cost of the venture may deter some travellers.

You may wonder why I have included it at all. The reason is that, despite these deterents, this trip is so stunning, the variety of scenery so spectacular and the change in cultures and climes so extraordinary that I would urge anyone to move heaven and earth to give it a try.

Start by checking all the various imponderables with your travel agent in Kathmandu (**Adventure Travel Nepal**, PO Box 242, Kathmandu. Tel: 223-328, 415-995; Telex: 2216; Fax: 414-075). Make sure you have a re-entry visa to Nepal as well as a Chinese visa for Tibet. Equip yourselves with warm clothes, as the winds on the arid Tibet plateau will be cold throughout the year. Take sunglasses, suncream and scarves to protect yourself from the glare and the dust. Buy extra food and chocolate to sustain you in case you don't like what the hotel offers.

Tibetan family

Although in one day's drive you travel from Zhangmu at 6,930ft (2,112m) to the highest pass over 16,000ft (5,000m), because you return to sleep at Zhangmu at the end of the day there is little danger of full-blown altitude sickness. However, you may find you suffer temporary symptoms such as giddiness, headaches and nausea. To help minimize such ill effects be sure to take with you plenty of liquid to drink (but not alcohol) and move slowly and cautiously in the high, thin air.

The drive on the **Arniko Highway** to the border will take you about four hours. The route is very beautiful, winding through the terraced hills and the great valleys of the **Sun Koshi River** and its tributary, the **Bhote Koshi**. Set off early, armed with a packed lunch, and be prepared for delays at the border. On the way you will pass through the Nepali towns of **Barabise** and **Tatopani** where you will notice remnants of landslides. Nepal immigration is at **Kodari**, and soon after, the first Chinese soldiers on the **Friendship Bridge** come into view.

The no-man's-land between the Nepal checkpost and entry into Tibet on the edge of the sprawling trading depot of **Zhangmu** (also known confusingly as **Khasal**) is a steep hillside above the Bhote Khosi. The **Zhangmu Hotel** is immediately after the checkpost on the left. Also confusing is the fact that Chinese time is three hours and fifteen minutes ahead of Nepalese time.

Leave as early as you can the next morning and be prepared for one of the most extraordinary journeys of your life. There is something magical about leaving the lush Nepalese alpine scenery, penetrating the Himalayan range through the spectacular, deep gorge of the Bhote Koshi, and emerging into another world, that of ancient Tibet. You are now in the rain shadow, north of the white peaks of the great mountains that only yesterday you had seen from the south. Guarded by ruined *dzongs* (forts), the arid plateau is tilled by yaks, while nomads tend their herds of sheep and goats and the medieval-looking villages of Tibet huddle against the harsh glare of the elements.

North of the small town of **Nyalam**, perched at the head of the gorge, is the village of **Zhonggang** and the recently rebuilt cave monastery of **Phenkyeling**. This is said to be one of the cave retreats of Milarepa, the 11th-century hermit. The road climbs across two passes, the **Thong La** (16,811ft/5124m) and the **Lalung La** (16,665ft/5,050m), both crowned with stone *chortens* (cairns) and prayer flags, proffered in thanks for a safe journey.

View from Phenkyeling

The drama of the vista of the many-coloured mountains unfold in a majestic panorama. **Xixabangma** (26,286ft/8,012m), which is also known as **Gosainthan**, is the only 26,000-ft (8,000-m) mountain that is completely within Tibet, and can be seen to the west.

After reaching the stone village of **Tingri**, you will be able to see the north faces of **Everest** (29,029ft/8,848m) and **Cho Oyu** (26,906ft/8,201m) across the plains against a cobalt sky. From here it is another two days' drive to **Lhasa**.

After spending a second night at the Zhangmu Hotel, return as soon as Chinese and Nepalese border formalities can be completed. Lunch in the comparative sophistication of the **Dhulikhel Mountain Resort**, amidst the green and gold of Nepal's countryside. From here it is barely an hour's journey back to Kathmandu – and the 'real world'.

A **pleasant alternative**, if logistics and permissions to Tibet are not forthcoming, is to drive from Kathmandu down the Arniko Highway as far as you wish towards the Tibetan border. Return to spend the night in the private chalets of the Dhulikhel Mountain Resort (PO Box 2303, Kathmandu. Tel: 220-031 and 216-930; no fax) enjoying the views, walks and comfort that this penultimate line establishment has to offer.

Right, a Tibetan drukpa, nomad

Eating Out

Unlike other Asian countries, Nepali cuisine is nothing to write home about. Based on similar principles as north Indian cooking, the ordinary people of Nepal live on rice, *dahl* (lentils), curried vegetables, and eat meat usually only during festivals. True Nepali specialities are found only in private houses, so be sure to accept an invitation if offered. It is curious that Nepal's isolation did not spawn more regional specialities, especially as the Kathmandu Valley produces such superb vegetables in its fertile fields. However, there are now several restaurants that serve Nepali and Newari food, though their menus are usually combined with Indian or Tibetan dishes.

There are other cuisines on offer, including Chinese, Japanese, Italian and English. Prices in Nepal are generally much lower than elsewhere. Outside Kathmandu and Patan it is difficult to find appealing food, so on a day outing carry something from the bakeries or Thamel delicatessens, or a packed lunch from your hotel.

Produced in Nepal are a variety of alcoholic drinks including good beer, rum, vodka and gin and more dubious whisky and brandy.

Apples and oranges in Patan

Yoghurt is sold in earthernware bowls

Try the local *raksi* (distilled rice or wheat) or *chhang* (fermented grain, usually barley or millet) if offered in a private house. Imported wines are available only at the hotels and better restaurants, at often prohibitive prices. Bottled soft drinks such as Coke and Pepsi, and mineral water are widely available.

A drink in the bars of Thamel before dinner is always fun if you wish to people-watch – try **Spam's Place** and **Tom & Jerry's** for local colour and the **Rumdoodle** for trekkers and climbers. Otherwise night life is minimal, despite a couple of desultory discotheques in the hotels. Restaurants rarely stay open after 10.30pm – except the casinos at **Annapurna** and **Soaltee Oberoi hotels**, which never close.

Nepali Restaurants

BHANCHA GHAR
Kamaladi
Tel: 225-172
Nepali food in a converted old house designed for tourists but with considerable charm.

GHAR E KABAB
Hotel Annapurna, Durbar Marg
Tel: 221-711
Terrific Indian kebabs and curries with live sitar music at night. Be sure to book ahead, as this is probably the most popular restaurant in town.

HIMALCHULI
Hotel Soaltee Oberoi
Tel: 272-550
Nepali and Indian specialities with a cultural show at 8pm nightly.

NAACH GHAR
Hotel Yak & Yeti, Durbar Marg
Tel: 411-436
Nepali and Indian food in a beautiful neo-classical ballroom. Cultural show on Sundays and Tuesdays. If there are more than 10 people, have the hotel arrange a special dinner in one of their amazing Rana reception rooms.

SUN KOSI
Tindhara
Tel: 226-520
Good traditional Nepali and Tibetan cuisine in a cosy brick interior. Ask for the homemade achars (chutneys).

Brass pots sell by the weight

Other Options

AL FRESCO
Hotel Soaltee Oberoi
Tel: 272-550
Italian cuisine in a lively taverna atmosphere. Pizzas and desserts are especially good and the pasta in a walnut cream sauce is delicious.

FUJI
Kantipath
Tel: 225-272
Authentic Japanese food in picturesque Rana cottage complete with stucco columns and moat.

HIM THAI
Thamel
Tel: 229-230
Imaginative Thai cooking in a Rana oasis in the midst of the action.

KC'S
Thamel
Tel: 414-387
An old favourite hangout which retains its atmosphere and value.

KUSHI FUJI
Durbar Marg
Good value fixed lunches at this Japanese restaurant.

MOUNTAIN CITY CHINESE
Malla Hotel, Lekhnath Marg
Tel: 410-320
The best Chinese food in town with authentic Sichuan cooks and professional service.

MIKE'S BREAKFAST
Durbar Marg,
off the Yak and Yeti road.
Tel: 227-834
Serves huge breakfasts, soups and quiches in a charming Rana cottage garden. Good music and good value.

SHAMBALA GARDEN CAFE
Shangrila Hotel, Lazimpath
Tel: 412-999
Elegant outdoor dining amidst Nepali lamps, also great for lunch. French cuisine and spectacular pastries.

Shopping

Kathmandu is a treasure trove of opportunities for shoppers, but beware of the cheap trinkets that tend to look like the junk they are when you return home. It is expected that you will bargain, except in the smart shops, and even then it is worth a try. As a general rule, if you like it and can afford it, buy it – you may never find the same thing again. The main shops are in **Thamel**, **Durbar Marg** and **Jawalakhel** but you will find temptations wherever you go.

Nepalese Handicrafts

One positive aspect of the huge tourist boom in Nepal is the improvement in locally made handicrafts. For a wide selection of what is available call in at **Dhukuti** and **Hastakala** (Handicrafts) in Patan just across the bridge. All the crafts on sale in these attractive shops are made in Nepal by disadvantaged groups; proceeds go to charity.

Look out for handspun fabrics from Kirtipur, brass candlesticks from Patan, woodcarvings in the form of traditional window photo frames and beautiful handmade paper and cards from Bhaktapur. The **Mahaguthi** shops, one just down the hill in Patan and one in Durbar Marg have similar arrangements. **Pasal**, in an arcade off

Wooden masks and household implements

Puppets and masks in Bhaktapur

Durbar Marg, sells especially clever gift items of imaginative local and regional decorative items, useful household goods and toys.

Beautiful religious scroll paintings hung in silk are best bought in Bhaktapur where they are painted. Look in the shops in **Tamaudi Tole** leading down from the Durbar Square, check for fine detailed work and gold leaf. Also look in the **Indigo Gallery** in Thamel. Multi-coloured masks and dancing puppets can be found in Bhaktapur. Also check out the terra-cotta animals at Thimi although you would need to be very taken by them to hand-carry them home.

Patan craftsmen are famous for their metalwork, and silver and goldsmiths ply their trade using tools and methods that have hardly changed in centuries. Especially interesting is the 'lost wax' method of casting bronze which can be seen at **Nepal Traditional Crafts** (Tel: 521-071) in Patan, on the right-hand side, up the hill past the Himalaya Hotel.

Nepal Carpets

Now a major export industry, these beautiful handmade wool carpets are world famous and good value in Nepal, as you might expect. Choose from a dazzling selection from the shops in **Jawalakhel**, or **Thamel**. They mostly measure 3ft by 6ft (1 by 2 meters) and reflect traditional Tibetan designs. The soft pastel colours are very popular, though not 'naturally dyed' as the shopkeepers would have you believe.

Pashmina Shawls

Wool and mixed wool shawls make excellent gifts. They are available from shops in Thamel but the best selection can be found at **Everest Pashmina Arts** in Kamal Pokhari (opposite the old Lhotse Hotel). Made from the finest goat wool, the pure white ones are the most expensive.

Jackets and Sweaters

Less fine but quite fun and again good for gifts are the multi-coloured sweaters available in Thamel. Patchwork jackets sold in the road on which the Yak and Yeti Hotel stand are amusing, and the wool waistcoats and crossover jackets made from the monk's wool cloth in **Bodhnath** (sold in a shop on the west side of the stupa) are wonderful.

Silk

Nepal silk is not yet up to international standards but you will be tempted by the delightful hand-painted Chinese silk outfits and scarfs in **Mandala** and **Tara**, elegant boutiques in Durbar Marg and Keshar Mahal respectively.

Gurkha Khukris

The genuine *khukris*, traditional curved knives of Nepal, are for sale in the **Tiger Tops shop** in Durbar Marg, hand made by British Gurkha soldiers in their army workshops. Beware of poor-quality imitations being sold on the streets.

Jewellery

No major precious stones are found in Nepal but you will find good silver-work bracelets and tiny animals in traditional Nepali filigree designs, sometimes inlaid with small pieces of coral or turquoise.

The Sherpas and Tibetans value the dark red coral highly. Turquoise should be bright blue-green. Both are traded from Tibet and are not cheap. Look for pretty silver bangles and earrings; unique to Nepal are the plaited bangles of three metals – copper, brass and silver (or iron) – popular with those who suffer from arthritis. Most convenient are the **Durbar Marg** or **New Road jewellers**. Try the excellent **Gem Palace** at the Yak and Yeti Hotel or **Noor Gems** near the Woodlands Hotel in Durbar Marg for a selection of what is available. Enjoy making your own combinations of multi-coloured glass beads in the **Bead Market**, in Indrachowk.

Paintings

B B Thapa, in his shop to the right beside the big tree opposite SATA in Jawalakhel, offers an enchanting range of Kathmandu Valley and Nepal view paintings in the primitive style normally associated with Sherpan or Tibetan fresco painters. He also has a selection in his shop outside the Soaltee Oberoi.

Antiques and Art Objects

Kathmandu is a treasure trove for collectors. Glory in a galaxy of superb old Tibetan carpets, precious *thangkas*, Chinese embroideries, porcelain and jade, Bhutanese dress pieces, coral and turquoise jewellery, gold and silver ritual art objects and fine Nepali bronzes.

It is no longer easy to find bargains and prices tend to be index-linked. Be aware of the local restrictions for exporting, which require certificates for some antiques; get the shopkeeper to help you. Recommended are the **Tibet Ritual Art Gallery** and the **Potala Gallery**, on the first floors in Durbar Marg and the **T T Gallery** in Keshar Mahal, but keep your eyes open in Bodhnath.

By appointment only, call **Barbara Adams** (Tel: 417-617) to see her beautiful collection of antiques and ethnic fabrics for sale in her home in Naxal.

Calendar of Special Events

Nepal is known as the land of festivals. Here, in the shadow of the mountain gods, celebrations are so frequent that the festivals often overlap each other. There are more than 50 such occasions a year, with as many as 120 days set aside to be observed. Most are linked to one or both of the country's great religions, Hinduism and Buddhism. Nepali's celebrate enthusiastically, and you are welcome to take part.

Festival dates vary from year to year because of the lunar calendar. Many are determined only after complex astrological calculations and as some festivals take place over a period of several days, it is usually difficult to know in advance which day festivities will take place, or where. The uncertainty is even considered part of the mystery.

This list will give you a guideline, but you should check dates with your hotel or travel agent when you arrive in Kathmandu.

Royal escort accompanies the King

MAGH (JANUARY/FEBRUARY)

Magh Sankranti. Marked with ritual bathing, even though it often falls on the coldest day of the year, this festival marks the passing of the inauspicious winter month of Pousch and rejoices that spring is at hand.
Maha Snan. Celebrates the holy bath given to Shiva, when he is bathed in yoghurt and honey and dressed anew.
Basant Panchami. The Festival of Spring is also the festival of Saraswati, goddess of learning. Students about to take exams and hundreds of devotees flock to the Saraswati shrine at Swayambhunath. The King attends ceremonies at Hanuman Dhoka to offer prayers for a good harvest. A most auspicious day to get married or to introduce children to the alphabet.
Magh Purnima. The full moon (*purnima*) marks the beginning of the month in which Parvati is worshipped at her shrines.

PHALGUN (FEBRUARY/MARCH)

Shivaratri. This great festival celebrating the birthday of Shiva is the time to be at Pashupatinath. A colourful crowd of literally thousands of devotees, *yogis* and *sadhus*, or holy ascetics, from all over the Indian subcontinent gather to line up to make offerings to Lord Pashupati, keep a night time vigil with bonfires and bathe at dawn in the Bagmati River.
Democracy Day or **King Tribhuvan Jayanti**. The statue of King Tribhuvan is garlanded in a procession to Tripureshwar.
Losar or **Tibetan New Year**. One of the most beautiful festivals, usually coincides within a few days of Chinese New Year. The third day of the otherwise family and house-oriented holiday is the time for celebrating at Bodhnath. Everyone dresses in their best clothes and jewellery and joins in the celebrations where new prayer flags are hung, the Dalai Lama's portrait paraded and one of the great moments of the year takes place as hundreds of Tibetans throw *tsampa* or barley flour into the air accompanied by a great roar of welcome to the New Year. Dancing takes place in the evening at monasteries around the stupa at Bodhnath.

Losar at Bodhnath

Holi or **Phagu**. Kathmandu Durbar Square is where this rowdy festival of colour and fertility is celebrated with the raising of a 25ft (7.5m) *chir* or bamboo pole, decked with streamers, burned at the end of the week. Wear old clothes as you are most likely to be sprayed with coloured water by over enthusiastic kids.

CHAITRA MARCH/APRIL

Seto or Rath. For four days during early evening, the guardian deity of the Seto (White) Machhendra is pulled in a towering chariot through the streets of Kathmandu. The vehicle which stands on wheels six feet (1.8m) in diameter is finally transported back to the shrine at Asan Tole on a small palanquin. Before this, on each night, the chariot stops at specific places where residents tend to the image.

Ghorajatra. Celebrated by horse races and gymnastics attended by the King, this horse festival has become a military pageant and draws crowds to the Tundhikhel.

Pase Chare. Coincides with Ghorajatra. After the horsemanship displays, the demon Gurumpa is carried to the Tundhikhel in a midnight procession.

Chaitra Dasain. Ritual offerings and sacrifices are made to Durga, exactly six months away from her great festival of Desain.

BAISAKH APRIL/MAY

Bisket. Bhaktapur is the place to be for this exciting and rousing festival which lasts for a week and celebrates the slaying of two demon serpents. A frenetic tug of war at dusk determines who shall have the honour of dragging a huge chariot conveying Bhadrakali and Bhairav through the streets of the city. Spectacular masked dancing and the felling of a long pole, commemorating victory during the great battle of Mahabharata mark the beginning of the Nepalese New Year.

Bal Kumari Jatra. The New Year is marked at Thimi with torch-lit processions honouring the Bal Kumari, a consort of Bhairav.

New Year prayer flags, Bodhnath

Mata Tirtha Shan or **Mothers' Day**. Persons whose mothers have died during the year must ritually bathe at this temple near Thankot. Living mothers are offered gifts.

Buddha Jayanti. Lord Buddha's birthday is celebrated at all Buddhist shrines, particularly Bodhnath and Swayambhunath.

JESHTHA MAY/JUNE

Sithinakha or **Kumar Shasthi**. Jaisedewal, south of Kathmandu Durbar Square, will be thronged with people celebrating the birthday of Kumar, son of Shiva.

Seto Machhendranath Festival

ASHADH JUNE/JULY

Tulsi Bijropan. This women's festival of fasting and purification involves planting the sacred *tulsi* plant, a close relative of common basil.

Gokarana Aunshi or **Fathers Day**. Celebrated by ritual bathing at the Gokarna Mahadev for those whose father has died in the past year. Living fathers are honoured with gifts.

SHRAWAN
JULY/AUGUST

Bhoto Jatra. Astrologers fix the exact time. The culmination of the several-month long procession of the Rato (Red) Machhendranath chariot since it set off from Pulchok in April, this important Patan festival is designed to ensure a good monsoon for crops.

The bejewelled waistcoat or *bhoto*, supposedly belonging to the serpent king, is displayed at Jawalakhel in the presence of the royal family. Once every 12 years (the next time is 2003) the chariot is dragged painstakingly all the way to Bungamati.

Ghanta Karna. The Night of the Devil is traditionally the last day for rice planting. The evil demon was outwitted by a frog and children collect coins to pay for his funeral.

Nag Panchami. *Nagas*, or the sacred serpents, are worshipped and pictures can be seen displayed above many doorways.

Raksha Bandhan or **Janai Purne**. Every Brahman and Chhetri must renew their *munja*, or sacred thread on this day after first taking a ritual bath in holy water.

The Kumbeshwar Temple in Patan is the place to be, as the water in the tanks there supposedly come from the sacred Gosainkund Lake, high in Helambu. The beautiful gold and silver *linga*, usually kept in the temple, are displayed on this day on a platform in the middle of the tank, reached only along a narrow plank.

Gai Jatra. An epic love of a king and queen is celebrated in this festival, which is more like a carnival. Families in which deaths have occurred in the previous year will send cows or children dressed as cows to frolic and sing in the Durbar Squares of Kathmandu, Patan and Bhaktapur to assist their deceased's entry into heaven.

Newari New Year

Krishna Jayanti. Birthday of the beloved god Krishna is celebrated in Patan Durbar Square.

BHADRA
AUGUST/SEPTEMBER

Tij. This colourful women's festival has groups of red sari-clad ladies singing in high spirits in the streets on their way to ritually bathe in the Bagmati River at Pashupatinath.

Indra Jatra. Probably the most spectacular of all Valley festivals. Torchlit processions and dancing to honour Indra, the god of rain, are held in this eight-day celebration which centres on the Kathmandu Durbar Square.

On the third day the *Kumari*, or Living Goddess, is paraded in a special chariot and worshipped by the King himself. Masks of Bhairav decorate the city and local beer pours forth from the mouths of these masks to refresh the local revellers.

ASHWIN
SEPTEMBER/OCTOBER

Dasain or **Durga Puja**. This ten-day festival is celebrated all over Nepal, honouring bountiful fertility and the conquest of evil. Normal life comes to a standstill as everyone attends their religious and family duties.

On *Phulpati*, the day of flowers, there is a procession to Hanuman Dhoka attended by the King. On the eighth and ninth days there are massive numbers of ritual animal sacrifices, for every tool that is used during the year must be blessed. Shrines all over the country literally run with blood. On the final day the palace is opened for all who wish to line up to receive a *tika* from the hands of the King or Queen.

Gai Jatra

KARTIK
OCTOBER/NOVEMBER

Tihar, or **Diwali,** and **Lakshmi Puja**. The Festival of Lights starts with honouring the crow, the dog and the cow. The fourth day coincides with Newari New Year. On the fourth and fifth evenings Laksmi, the goddess of wealth and prosperity, is enticed into the home by lights. Thousands of oil lamps and candles adorn doors, windows and balconies. Brothers are feted by their sisters on the last day and honoured with elaborate *tikas* and garlands.
Haribodhini Ekadasi. This most auspicious *Ekadasi* (the eleventh day of each lunar fortnight, there are 24 in a year) welcomes Vishnu back from his long summer sleep. Join worshippers at Budhanilkanth where festivities culminate as fasting devotees conclude the pilgrimage to his temples of Changu Narayan, Bisankhu Narayan, Sekh Narayan and Ichangu Narayan.
HM The Queen's Birthday. The Queen receives a procession of well-wishers who visit the palace at Durbar Marg.

MARGA/MANGSIR
NOVEMBER/DECEMBER

Yomarhi Punhi. The Newari rice festival is celebrated at Panauti, where the family paddy store is blessed and rice cakes called *yomarhi* are prepared.

PAUSH
DECEMBER/JANUARY

Mahendra Jayanti or **Constitution Day**. Garlands are laid on the statue of King Mahendra in Durbar Marg.
Birendra Jayanti (The King's Birthday). Well-wishers at Durbar Marg bring birthday offerings to the King on this national holiday.
Prithvi Jayanti. The statue of King Prithvi Narayan Shah opposite Singha Durbar is garlanded and his photograph paraded through the city.

Festival dancing

Practical Information

TRAVEL ESSENTIALS

When to Visit

October to April is the best time to visit Nepal. However, being the most popular, this is also the most crowded time. The cold clear winter months of December and January are good for mountain views, despite misty mornings and an invigorating evening chill. However, trekking at higher altitudes can be impossible from January through February, as passes may be blocked by snow and there is a danger of avalanches.

The next busiest, and in many ways the best months, are February and March with spring flowers and gentle temperatures. Late April and May can be hot and hazy and it is best to avoid the monsoon rains from June to September if you are planning to trek or visit the lowland national parks.

In the Valley, however, this can be one of the prettiest times with only intermittent rain, lush green rice fields, wonderful light effects and very few other visitors.

Visas

Visas valid for 15 days can be bought on arrival at Kathmandu airport for US$15 by all foreign nationals except British passport holders, for whom the fee is £20. To avoid unnecessary delay, be sure you have passport-sized photographs and the right change.

Visas valid for 30 days can be obtained from a Nepalese Embassy prior to arrival. All tourist visas can be extended at the Department of Immigration in Thamel, Tel: 412-337 (open 10am–5pm daily but Friday until 3pm, closed Saturday) for up to three months, upon proof that at least US$20 per day has been exchanged for the duration of the visa.

If you are planning to leave and return, be sure to ask for a multi-entry visa. Trek permits must be obtained by visitors planning to trek or travel to areas other than the Kathmandu Valley, Pokhara or the Terai.

Vaccinations

Vaccinations against typhoid, hepatitis (gamma globulin) and meningitis are recommended. Make sure your routine tetanus and polio inoculations are up to date. Yellow fever vaccinations are essential if arriving from an infected area. Cholera shots are not required.

Money Matters

Nepalese rupees are the monetary unit and the official rate of exchange fluctuates against other currencies. At time of press the rate was Rs 50 to US$1 but check the *Rising Nepal*, where rates are published daily on the back page.

Money can be changed in the banks and hotels and the exchange counter at the airport. Beware of the black market as hard currency is in high demand. Keep all Foreign Exchange Encashment Receipts as these are necessary for visa extensions and changing back excess rupees on departure.

It is illegal to export or import Nepalese currency. All airline, hotel and travel agency payments must be made in foreign exchange by foreigners. American Express, Mastercard and Visa are widely accepted.

Clothing

Your wardrobe will depend on what you are planning to do in Nepal but generally only the most casual clothes are required. Safari-style cottons, modest skirts, jeans and comfortable track shoes are ideal

with a warm sweater and jacket for cold winter evenings.

Bring sunglasses for daytime and rely on a local umbrella if it rains, which is seldom except during the monsoon. If you are trekking or river running, consult an equipment list for specialist gear.

Electricity

Electrical outlets are rated at 220 volts/50 cycles though some fluctuation is not unusual. Power cuts are common. Big hotels have their own generators. Bring a small flashlight.

Airport Tax

A departure tax of Rs 600 is charged per person on all international flights except to SAARC countries which is Rs 500. A tax of Rs 30 is levied on some (not all) domestic flights.

GETTING ACQUAINTED

Government and Geography

Nepal is a constitutional monarchy headed by His Majesty King Birendra Bir Bikram Shah Dev. Following demonstrations and riots, the palace announced on 8 April 1990 the lifting of the legal ban on political parties and on 9 November 1990 a new constitution was proclaimed.

The 1994 elections were won by the Communist Party of Nepal under Prime Minister Man Mohan Adhi Kami. Since September 1995 Nepal has been ruled by a coalition cabinet under Prime Minister Sher Bahadur Deuba.

The King (born 28 December 1945) and Queen Aishwarya Rajya Lakshmi Devi Shah (born 7 November 1949) have three children; the older, His Royal Highness Crown Prince Dipendra (born 27 June 1971) is heir to the throne. Nepal is the only Hindu monarchy in the world.

Over 90 percent of the 19 million population of Nepal are engaged in agriculture. Fifty percent are under the age of 21 and the population is growing at the annual rate of 2.6 percent.

As they are subsistence farmers, indus-

triously carving out a living from small plots on terraced hillsides, the annual per capita income of US$160 looks more alarmingly low than it is.

Development is hampered by lack of roads and infrastructure in this largely mountainous land which, in only 100 miles (160km) goes from the highest point on earth, Mount Everest, known in Nepal as Sagarmatha, 29,028ft/8,848m to the lowland Terai less than 350ft (100m) above sea level.

About the same size as England or New Zealand, Nepal stretches 553 miles (885km) from east to west and has a total land area of 56,139 sq miles (145,391 sq km).

Health care and literacy figures are amongst the world's worst and Nepal is largely dependant on foreign aid for its economic development. Tourism and handmade wool carpet exports are the largest foreign exchange earners.

Kathmandu, the capital, is at an altitude of 4,400ft (1,350m) and has a population of about 500,000, with almost one million people making the Kathmandu Valley their home.

Climate

Nepal has an extreme variety of climates, from the eternal snows of the Himalaya to the tropical lowlands.

Few capitals enjoy as many hours of sunshine as the Kathmandu Valley, which has three seasons:

Winter: October to March, 10°–25°C (50°–77°F), with cold nights dropping to almost freezing and a morning mist due to the rapidly rising daytime temperatures. Clear sparkling sunny days.

Spring: April to mid-June, 11°–30°C (52°–86°F), with warm, sometimes hazy days and occasional evening thunder storms, the nights are pleasantly cool.

Monsoon: June to September, 19°–36°C (66°–97°F), intermittent violent downpours (often only at night) create some flooding and landslides, and keep the temperature down and the humidity high.

Time

Nepal is five hours 45 minutes ahead of GMT and 15 minutes ahead of Indian Standard Time.

Calendars

Five different calendars are used simultaneously in Nepal. The official one used by the government is the lunar Bikram Samat calendar which started counting the days on 23 Feb 57 BC. Hence 1993 is 2050 of the Bikram era. However, the familiar Gregorian calendar is widely used. Traditional calendars include the Nepal Samat, established in AD879–880, the Shaka Samat, established AD77, and the Tibetan calendar, Bhot Byalo, established 127BC.

The Nepalese year which begins in mid-July, is 365 days long with 12 months ranging in length from 29 to 32 days, depending on solar movement. These months are: Baisakh (31 days), Jesth (31 days), Asadh (32 days), Srawan (32 days), Bhadra (31 days), Ashwin (30 days), Kartik (30 days), Marga (29 days), Poush

(30 days), Magha (29 days), Falgun (30 days), Chaitra (30 days).

Hours of Business

Government offices are open from 10am to 5pm, Sunday through Friday. They close at 4pm during the three winter months and early on Fridays at 3pm.

Banks open at 10am and close at 2pm except Friday when they close at 12 noon. Saturday is the only rest day in Nepal although most of the shops remain open every day until 7–8pm. Only embassies and international organisations have a two-day weekend.

Culture and Customs

Although every visitor is immediately struck by the charm and smiling friendliness of the Nepali people, avoid inadvertently offending your hosts and keep the following in mind. Both men and women can go about almost everywhere with confidence but keep your wallet out of sight and your bag zipped up.

If you are approached or hassled by the curious, smiling patiently usually gets better results from these proud people than losing your cool. Rarely do people mind being photographed, but it is polite to stop if they do.

Nepalis are on the whole very tolerant of tourist behavior, but respect in temples and shrines is expected – be ready to remove your shoes. The traditional Indian greeting, Namaste, literally translated as 'I salute all divine qualities in you', should be spoken while raising the hands in a prayer-like gesture. The King is regarded with genuine reverence as an incarnation of the Hindu god, Vishnu, so all references to the royal family must be suitably respectful.

Never point with a finger and specially not with your feet, never touch the top of anyone's head and never give or receive anything in your left 'polluted' hand – best is to offer and receive with both hands.

Tipping

It is customary to tip about 10 percent in restaurants, hotels and taxis, though not mandatory. Give 5 rupees to a porter who helps with your bags. What seems little to most is not insignificant when compared to local salaries. However do refrain from giving sweets and money to every child who asks.

Tourist Information and Maps

Rely on guide books; there are many. Recommended are *Insight Cityguide: Kathmandu Valley* and *Insight Guide: Nepal*, both published by Apa Publications and widely available in the many bookshops in town. The informative *Nepal Traveller* magazine may be handed to you free at the airport..

GETTING AROUND

Private Cars

The most convenient, reliable and time-effective way to get around is with a private car and guide, which can be booked through a travel agent or arranged through your hotel. If you stay within the rim of the Valley, it will cost you about US$50 for the whole day. If you are satisfied a Rs 50 tip is customary.

Taxis

Taxis are available to go most places and have black registration plates with white numbers; private cars have white numbers on red plates. Make sure their meters are working and be prepared to pay a 10 percent fuel surcharge.

Bicycles

A great way to see the Valley is by bicycle, especially the new mountain bikes, which are ideal for exploring the dirt roads of the Valley. Ordinary bicycles cost as little as Rs 10 a day (from the rental shops in Asan and Thamel) but mountain bikes are worth the extra. **Himalayan Mountain Bikes** , PO Box 2769, Kathmandu, tel: 413632 or 418733; fax: 415632. You can get information from their office in Thamel, near Kathmandu Guesthouse.

Walking

You should be prepared to do a lot of walking if you want to taste the real flavour of the Valley, absorb its people, their culture and way of life. Most of the interesting sights have to be reached and explored on foot. Leave the main roads and stroll at a leisurely pace through the rice and mustard fields. You can expect to be safe everywhere you go and will find the Nepalese people even more friendly off the beaten track.

Public Transport

Buses, trams, three-wheeled scooters (*tempos*) and bicycle-rickshaws all ply the streets of Kathmandu. They are all slow, noisy and fairly uncomfortable but they are a cheap way of getting around.

WHERE TO STAY

Hotels and Lodges

The prices below are for room only at time of press and do not include service charges (10 percent) or government tax which varies from 12–15 percent depending on the category. The star ratings awarded by the Department of Tourism are quantitative rather than qualitative, and this list is by no means exhaustive. Those marked with (*) officially have no star rating. There are plenty of lodges and guesthouses for less than US$10 to choose from in Thamel.

The following symbols indicate price ranges for a double room. $=under 50; $$=US$50–100; $$$=US$100–150.

Five-star

ANNAPURNA
Durbar Marg
Tel: 221-711, 223-602, Fax: 225-236
Now run by the Taj Group from India, this central hotel was the first five-star in town. 140 rooms, pool, tennis, several restaurants $$$

EVEREST
Baneswar
Tel: 220567, Fax: 226-088
162 rooms, pool, tennis, disco, restaurants. Wonderful view from the roof. $$$

SOALTEE OBEROI
Tahachal
Tel: 275-550, Fax: 272-205
The best hotel in town, with extensive fa-

cilities, recent renovations, good restaurants and spectacular 'regal' suites built for the South Asian (SAARC) Heads of State. $$$

YAK AND YETI
Durbar Marg
Tel: 413-999, 228-255, Fax: 227-782
Excellently located, this historic home of the great Boris Lissanevitch, founder of Nepal's tourism, is part Rana palace. Pool, tennish, sauna. $$$

Four-star

DWARIKA'S KATHMANDU VILLAGE*
Battisputali
Tel: 470-770, 472-328, Fax: 225-131
A wonderful Nepali antique woodcarving collection is incorporated into this imaginative family-run hotel. $$

HIMALAYA
Kupondole
Tel: 523-900/8, Fax: 523-909
Cool white marble, spacious rooms and a swimming pool with a view in this Japanese owned property. $$

KATHMANDU
Maharajgunj
Tel: 410-786, 418-494, Fax: 416-574
Rather cramped, with a small garden, but has an interesting brick atrium architecture. The plus point is that it serves good Indian food. $$

MALLA
Lekhnath Marg
Tel: 410-620, 410-968
Fax: 418-382
Well placed near the Royal Palace and other sights and well run. Has a charming garden and a restaurant serving the best Chinese food in town. $$

SHANGRILA*
Lazimpat
Tel: 412-999, Fax: 414-184
Lovely brick-built favourite with good food, great service and a glorious garden to ramble around in, and Elles, the best beauty salon in town. $$

SHANKER
Lazimpat
Tel: 412973, 410-551, Fax: 412-691
Former Rana Palace. Spectacular white neo-classical palace in huge gardens, well placed. $$

SHERPA
Durbar Marg
Tel: 227-000, Fax: 222-026
Centrally located with a pleasant roof. Indian and European food. $$

Three-star

NARAYANI
Patan
Tel: 521-711, 521-712, 521-408, Fax: 521-291
In the shadow of an Ashoka stupa, handy for Patan with a pleasant pool. $$

SUMMIT*
Kupondole Heights
Tel: 523-737, 524-694, Fax: 523-737
Lovely rooms, view and swimming pool in this pleasant hotel, though not very conveniently situated but quiet on account of this. $$

YELLOW PAGODA
Kantipath
Tel: 220-392, 220-337, Fax: 228-914
Known for its consistent service and very central location. $$

Two-star

AMBASSADOR
Lazimpat
Tel: 410-432, 414-432, Fax: 415-432
Convenient location. Run by the same management as the legendary Kathmandu Guest House. $

VAJRA
Bijeswari
Tel: 271-545, 272-719, Fax: 271-695
More a cultural experience than a hotel,

this wonderfully off-beat hotel's lack of facilities (for example, few adjoining bathrooms and few telephones in rooms) is more than made up for by its vibrancy and rooftop bar. $

One-star

KATHMANDU GUEST HOUSE
Thamel
Tel: 413-632, 418-733
US$17 (single) US$20 (double)
This is one of the best and certainly the most famous of the Thamel lodges, and a favourite with world travellers. Situated in the heart of the action, it is frequently fully booked. $

MANASLU
Lazimpat
Tel: 410-071, 413-470
Fax: 228-467
Friendly, quiet and central, this is a real 'find'. $

UTSE
Thamel
Tel: 228-952
Fax: 226-945
Clean, relatively quiet and convenient, boasting portraits of the Dalai Lama and John Major. $

TIBET GUEST HOUSE
Chetrapati
Tel: 214-383, 211-556
Near Thamel. Friendly, helpful and excellent value, this establishment comes well recommended. $

HEALTH AND EMERGENCIES

Hygiene

It is not uncommon for minor problems to occur and elementary hygiene precautions are in order. Never drink unboiled and untreated water and do not trust ice cubes anywhere except in the very best hotels. Avoid eating raw vegetables, peel all fruit and do not be tempted to eat anywhere except proper restaurants. Never walk barefoot and wash your hands frequently. 'Traveler's Tummy' should clear up after a few days but if it is severe and persistent, or interferes with your travel plans, get a stool test and medical assistance.

Medicine

Most medicines that you are likely to require are readily and cheaply available without a prescription. Look out for the well-known brands names manufactured under license in India but check the labels carefully as the contents may be different from those you are familiar with at home.

If you fall ill while in Nepal, do not rely on pharmacists when making a diagnosis but get proper medical assistance.

Clinics

There are Nepali doctors attached to all the big hotels. The **Nepal International Clinic** is in Hiti Durbar in Naxal (Tel: 412-842). Best of all is the American-staffed **CIWEC Clinic** in Baluwatar (opposite the Russian Embassy. (Tel: 410-983).

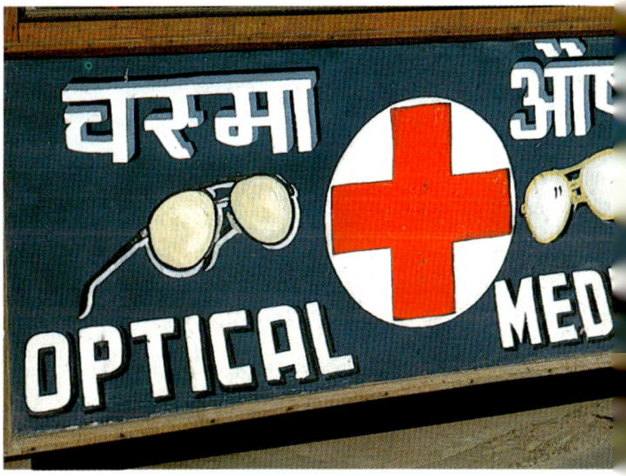

Hospitals

Some Kathmandu hospitals do have English-speaking staff butare not up to international standards. Where feasible, foreign visitors should try to reach the excellent hospital facilities in Bangkok, Thailand.

For accidents and emergencies, the best hospitals are:

Patan Hospital in Lagankhel, Patan. Tel: 521-048, 522-286, 522-278. This hospital is run by the United Mission to Nepal.

Teaching Hospital in Maharajgunj. Tel: 412-303, 412-404, 412-505, 412-808.

COMMUNICATION AND NEWS

Telecommunications and Postal Services

Main hotels have telephone, fax, telex and mail facilities. International direct dial telephone communications are satellite-linked and excellent. The country code is 977 and the Kathmandu area code is 1. To call abroad, dial the international access code 00, then the country code: Australia (61); France (33); Germany (49); Japan (81); Netherlands (31); Spain (34); UK (44); and US and Canada (1). Sprint, AT&T and MCI cards cannot be used here.

If you need to seek assistance, dial 186 for the international operator, 187 for calls to India, 180 for internal trunk calls and 197 for enquiries.

The Telecommunication Office in Tripureshwar deals with telephone calls and telexes if your hotel cannot. Its telex service is available only during government hours at the Central Telegraph office.

Fax has reached Nepal and is available in most hotels and offices. Public services in business centres are available in Thamel and Durbar Marg.

The mail service is less reliable so avoid having people send you letters during your visit. Mail cards or letters at your hotel or at the General Post Office (Tel: 211-037) at the junction of Kantipath and Kicha-Pokhari.

Media

There are several English newspapers and dozens in Nepali. The official English *Rising Nepal* has good coverage of foreign news and is widely read. Two weeklies, *The Independent* (published on Wednesdays) and *Sunday Despatch* are also recommended. *The International Herald Tribune* can be found one day late at newsstands and available weekly are *Time*, *Newsweek*, the *Far Eastern Economic Review*, *Asiaweek* and *India Today*.

Radio Nepal broadcasts two news bulletins in English daily at 8am and 8pm. Nepal Television arrived in 1986 and broadcasts daily from 7–8am and 7–10pm. Check the programmes daily in the *Rising Nepal* and bring a shortwave radio if you are addicted to international news.

SPECIAL INFORMATION

Nepali Language

There are as many tongues spoken in Nepal as there are races and almost as many dialects as there are valleys. The official language, Nepali, is derived from Pahori, an Indian language related to Hindi and uses the same writing system, Devanagari.

Nepali has also borrowed heavily from Sanskrit, an ancient scholarly language which has survived (like Latin) as a religious medium. Newari, the unique ancient language of the Newar people predominant in the Kathmandu Valley, uses three different alphabets and is the richest in literature and poetry.

In northern Nepal, the Tibetan language remains widespread and is the basis of dialects such as Sherpa and Thakali. English is widely spoken and understood, especially in government and tourism-related circles.

SPORTS

Other than the hotels, sports facilities are very limited for visitors, with the exception of the two golf courses that exist in the Valley, both nine holes and with browns instead of greens. Temporary members are welcome at the **Royal Nepal Golf Club** (Tel: 472-836) near the airport and at **Gokarna Safari Park** (Tel: 470-063) past Bodhnath in the King's Forest where you can even follow your round with an elephant ride. The five-star hotels all have swimming pools, tennis courts and some have health clubs. Paradoxically, skiing is out of the question, although a few mountaineering expeditions do it. The steepness of slopes and high snow line and altitude make skiing impractical.

Leisure is a concept unfamiliar to Nepalis who spend their spare time tending to family and religious commitments.

USEFUL INFORMATION

Key Telephone Numbers

Police Emergency	226-998
	226-999
Red Cross Ambulance	228-094
Patan Hospital	521-048
	522-286
	522-278
Teaching Hospital	412-303
	412-404
	412-505
	412-808
CIWEC Clinic	410-983
Nepal International Clinic	412-842
Fire Brigade	221-177
Telephone Enquiry	197
International Operator	186
Operator for India	187
Internal Trunk Calls	180

Credit Card Offices

AMERICAN EXPRESS
Durbar Marg
Tel: 226-172

MASTERCHARGE AND VISA
c/o Nepal Grindlays Bank
Kantipath
Tel: 228-473

International Organizations

FRENCH CULTURAL CENTER
Bagh Bazaar. Tel: 224-326

BRITISH COUNCIL
Kantipath. Tel: 221-305

GOETHE INSTITUTE
Ganabahal, Tel: 220-528

UNITED NATIONS
Pulchok. Tel: 523-200

US INFORMATION SERVICE
New Road. Tel: 223-893

Airlines

AIR FRANCE
Durbar Marg. Tel: 223-339

AIR INDIA
Kantipath. Tel : 211-730

BANGLADESH BIMAN
Durbar Marg. Tel: 222-544

BRITISH AIRWAYS
Durbar Marg. Tel: 222-266

CATHAY PACIFIC
Kanti Path. Tel: 226-765

CHINA SOUTH WEST AIRLINES
Kamaladi. Tel: 411-302

DRAGON AIR
Durbar Marg. Tel: 227-064

DRUK AIR
Durbar Marg. Tel: 225-166

EVEREST AIR
Durbar Marg. Tel: 229-412

INDIAN AIRLINES
Durbar Marg. Tel: 223-933

LUFTHANSA
Durbar Marg. Tel: 223-052

NECON AIR
Putali Sadak. Tel: 418-608

NEPAL AIRWAYS
Kamal Pokhari. Tel: 410-786

NORTHWEST AIRLINES
Lainchaur. Tel: 418-387

PAKISTAN INTERNATIONAL
Durbar Marg. Tel: 223-102

ROYAL NEPAL AIRLINES
New Road. Tel: 220-757

SINGAPORE AIRLINES
Durbar Marg. Tel: 220-759

THAI INTERNATIONAL
Durbar Marg. Tel: 224-917

TRANS WORLD AIRLINES
Kamaladi. Tel: 411-725

Travel Agencies

ADVENTURE TRAVEL NEPAL
Durbar Marg. Tel: 221-729
Lazimpat. Tel: 415-995

ANNAPURNA TRAVELS & TOURS
Durbar Marg. Tel: 222-339
Fax: 220-215

EVEREST EXPRESS
Durbar Marg. Tel: 220-759

GORKHA TRAVELS
Durbar Marg. Tel: 224-896

KATHMANDU TRAVELS & TOURS
Baltisputali. Tel: 224-536

MALLA TRAVELS
Malla Hotel. Tel: 410-635

MARCO POLO
Gyaneshwor. Tel: 414-192

NATRAJ TOURS & TRAVELS
Ghantaghar. Tel: 222-906

SHANKAR TRAVEL
Shankar Hotel. Tel: 412-465

TIGER TOPS
Durbar Marg, Kathmandu. Tel: 222-706
Lazimpat. Tel: 415-659

TRANS HIMALAYAN TOURS
Durbar Marg. 223-854

WORLD TRAVELS
Durbar Marg. Tel: 226-939

YETI TRAVELS
Durbar Marg. Tel: 221-234

Trekking Agencies

ABOVE THE CLOUDS TREKKING
Thamel. Tel: 416-923

AMA DABLAM TREKKING
Lazimpat. Tel: 410-219

ASIAN TREKKING
Tridevi Marg. Tel: 413-732

HIMALAYAN ADVENTURES
Lazimpat. Tel: 411-477

HIMALAYAN JOURNEYS
Kantipat. Tel: 226-626

HIMALAYAN ROVER TREK
Naxal. Tel: 412-667

INTERNATIONAL TREKKERS
Durbar Marg. Tel: 418-594

LAMA EXCURSIONS
Durbar Marg. Tel: 220-186

MOUNTAIN TRAVEL NEPAL
Naxal. Tel: 414-508

NATRAJ TREKKING
Kantipat. Tel: 226-644

NEPAL HIMAL
Baluwatar. Tel: 419-796

SHERPA COOPERATIVE TREKKING
Durbar Marg. Tel: 224-068

SHERPA TREKKING SERVICE
Durbar Marg. Tel: 224 068

TRANS HIMALAYAN TREKKING
Durbar Marg. Tel: 223-854

Foreign Missions in Nepal

AUSTRALIA
Bhat Bhateni. Tel: 411-578

BANGLADESH
Naxal. Tel: 414-943

BURMA (MYAMAR)
Pulchowk. Tel: 521-788

CHINA
Baluwatar. Tel: 411-740

FRANCE
Lazimpat. Tel: 412-332

GERMANY
Ganeshwar. Tel: 412-786

INDIA
Lainchaur. Tel: 410-900

ITALY
Baluwatar. Tel: 412-743

PAKISTAN
Pani Pokhari Tel: 410-565

RUSSIA
Baluwatar. Tel: 412-155

THAILAND
Thapathali. Tel: 213-910

UNITED KINGDOM
Lainchaur. Tel: 411-590, 414-588

USA
Pani Pokhari. Tel: 411-179

FURTHER READING

There are a number of excellent bookshops in Kathmandu, where you will find books on the region. They include **Himalayan Booksellers** with branches in Durbar Marg, Kantipath, Thamel; **Pilgrims Book Centre** in the depths of Thamel; **Educational Enterprises** in Kantipat opposite Bir Hospital; **Himalayan Book Centre** in Bag Bazaar; and the **Tibet Book Store** in Keshar Mahal underneath Coppers Restaurant.

General

Hagen, Toni. *Nepal: The Kingdom in the Himalayas*. Berne: Kummerly and Frey, 1980. Geographical study with many photos and maps. Hagen, who spent eight years surveying Nepal, was of the first persons to travel widely in the country.
Van Gruisen, Lisa. *Insight Cityguide: Kath-*

mandu Valley. Apa Publications, Singapore, 1990. In-depth survey of history and culture plus detailed descriptions of monuments in the Kathmandu Valley.

Peissel, Michel. *Tiger for Breakfast*. Hodder, London, 1966. The story of Boris Lissanevitch, who came to Kathmandu in 1951 and opened the first hotel, the Royal.

Suyin, Han. *The Mountain is Young*. Jonathon Cape, London, 1958. Charming novel capturing the heady atmosphere of Nepal in the 1950s.

People, Art and Culture

Anderson, Mary M. *Festivals of Nepal*. George Allen & Unwin, London, 1971.

Aran, Lydia. *The Art of Nepal*. Shahayogi Prakashan, Kathmandu, 1978. Mostly about the Kathmandu Valley with an accent on religion.

Bista, Dor Bahadur. *People of Nepal*. Ratna Pustak Bhandar, Kathmandu, 1974. Classic survey.

Natural History

Fleming, R.L. Sr, R.L. Fleming Jr and L.S. Bangdel. *Birds of Nepal*. Avalok, Kathmandu, 1979. Definitive work, good illustrations.

Inskipp, Carol. *A Birdwatcher's Guide to Nepal*. Bird Watchers Guides, England, 1988. Excellent and helpful guide.

McDougal, Charles. *The Face of the Tiger*. Rivington Books and Andre Deutsch, London, 1977. Classic work on the tiger by the Wildlife Director of Tiger Tops.

Polunin, Oleg and Stainton, Adam. *Concise Flowers of the Himalaya*. Oxford University Press, New Delhi, 1987. A standard work with beautiful illustrations.

Smith, Colin. *Butterflies of Nepal (Central Himalaya)*. Teopress, Bangkok, 1989. Scholarly standard work.

Storrs, Adrian & Jimmy. *Enjoy Trees: A simple guide to some of the shrubs found in Nepal*. Sahayogi Press, Kathmandu, 1987. Useful and practical handbook.

Trekking

Bezruschka, Stephen. *A Guide to Trekking in Nepal*. The Mountaineers, Seattle, 1981. Probably the best trekking guide.

Hillary, Sir Edmund. *Insight Topic: Sagarmatha*. Apa Publications, Singapore 1992. Unique collection of stunning photographs of the Everest collected as a fund-raising classic for the Himalayan Trust.

O'Connor, Bill. *The Trekking Peaks of Nepal*. Seattle: Cloudcap Press 1989 and England: Crowood Press. Useful maps.

Choegyal, Lisa. *Insight Guide: Nepal*. Apa Publications, Singapore 1990. Complete coverage of trekking, climbing, national parks, the Terai and Kathmandu Valley.

GLOSSARY

A

Ananda	Buddha's chief disciple.
Ananta	A huge snake whose coils created Vishnu's bed.
arak	A whisky fermented from potatoes or grain.
Asadh	The third month of the Nepalese year.
Ashwin	The sixth month of the Nepalese year.
Ashta Matrikas	The eight mother goddesses said to attend on Shiva.
Avalokiteshwara	A *bodhisattiva* regarded as the god of mercy in Mahayana Buddhist tradition, and as the compassionate Machhendra in Nepal.
avatar	An incarnation of a deity on earth.

B

bahal	A two-storey Buddhist monastery enclosing a courtyard.

bahil — A Buddhist monastery, smaller and simpler than a *bahal*.

Baisakh — First month of the Nepalese year.

Bajra Jogini — A Tantric goddess.

betel — A stimulating mixture of areca nut and white lime, wrapped in a betel leaf and chewed.

Bhadra — The fifth month of the Nepalese year.

Bhagavad-Gita — The most important Hindu religious scripture, in which the god Krishna spells out the importance of duty. It is contained in the *Mahabharata*.

Bhairav — The god Shiva in his most terrifying form.

Bhimsen — A deity worshipped for his strength and courage.

bodhisattiva — In Mahayana tradition, a person who has attained the enlightened level of Buddhahood, but has chosen to remain on earth to teach until others are enlightened.

Bon — The pre-Buddhist religion of Tibet, incorporating animism and sorcery.

Brahma — In Hindu mythology, the god of creation.

brahman — The highest Hindu caste, originally of priests.

C

Chaitra — The 12th and last month of the Nepalese year.

chaitya — A small stupa, sometimes containing a Buddhist relic, but usually holding mantras or holy scriptures.

chhang — A potent mountain beer of fermented grain, usually barley.

chhetri — The Hindu warrior caste, second in status only to *brahmans*.

chiya — Nepalese tea, brewed together with milk, sugar and spices.

chorten — A small Buddhist shrine usually in high mountain regions.

chowk — A palace or public courtyard.

crore — A unit of counting equal to 10 million.

D – F

Dalai Lama — The reincarnate high priest of Tibetan Buddhism and political leader of Tibetans around the world.

Dattatraya — A syncretistic deity variously worshipped as an incarnation of Vishnu, a teacher of Shiva, or a cousin of the Buddha.

Devi — (or *Maha Devi*) 'The great goddess'. Shiva's *shakti* in her many forms.

dhal — A lentil soup.

Dharma — Buddhist doctrine. Literally 'the path'.

dharmasala — A public rest house for travellers and pilgrims.

doko — A basket, often carried on the head by means of a strap.

dorje — A ritual sceptre or thunderbolt, symbol of the Absolute to Tantric Buddhists (also *vajra*).

Durga — Shiva's *shakti* in one of her most awesome forms.

dyochhen — A house enshrining protective Tantric deities and used for common worship.

Falgun — The 11th month of the Nepalese year.

G – H

gaine — A wandering, begging minstrel.

Ganesh — The elephant-headed son of Shiva and Parvati. He is worshipped as the god of good luck and the remover of obstacles.

Garuda — A mythical eagle, half human. The vehicle of Vishnu.

Gautama Buddha	The historical Buddha, born in Lumbini in the 6th century BC.
ghat	A riverside platform for bathing and cremation.
gompa	Tibetan Buddhist monastery.
Gorakhnath	Historically, an 11th-century yogi who founded a Shaivite cult; now popularly regarded as an incarnation of Shiva.
guthi	A communal Newar brotherhood, serving the purpose of mutual support for members and their extended families.
Hanuman	A deified monkey. Hero of the *Ramayana* epic, his is believed to bring success to armies.
hiti	A water conduit; a bath or tank with water spouts.

I – J

Indra	The god of rain.
Jagannath	Krishna, worshipped as 'Lord of the World'.
jatra	Festival.
Jesth	The second month of the Nepalese year.
jhankri	A shahman or sorcerer.
jogini	A mystical goddess.
jyapu	Newar farmer caste.

K

Kali	Shiva *shakti* in her most terrifying form.
karma	The cause and effect chain of actions, good and bad, from one life to the next.
Kartik	The seventh month of the Nepalese year.
khukhri	A traditional knife, long and curved, best known as the weapons of Gurkha soldiers.
Krishna	The eighth incarnation of Vishnu, worshipped for his activities on earth.
kumari	A young virgin regarded as a living goddess in Kathmandu Valley towns.

L

lakh	A unit equal to 100,000.
Lakshmi	The goddess of wealth and consort of Vishnu.
lama	A Tibetan Buddhist priest.
lingum	A symbolic male phallus, generally associated with Shiva; (plural:*linga*).

M

Machhendra	The guardian god of the Kathmandu Valley, guarantor of rain and plenty, who is enshrined as the Rato (Red) Machhendra in Patan and the Seto (White) Machhendra in Kathmandu.
Magha	The 10th month of the Nepalese year.
Mahabharata	An important Hindu epic.
Mahayana	A form of Buddhism prevalent in East Asia, Tibet and Nepal.
Maitreya	The future Buddha.
mandala	A sacred diagram envisioned by Tibetan Buddhists as an aid to meditation.
mandap	A roofless Tantric shrine made of brick or wood.
Manjushri	The legendary Buddhist patriarch of the Kathmandu Valley, now often regarded as the god of learning.
mantra	Sacred syllables chanted during meditation by Buddhists.
Marga	The eighth month of the Nepalese year.
math	A Hindu priest's house.
munja	The sacred thread worn by Brahman and Chettri males rom the time of puberty.

N

naga	Snake, especially a legendary or a deified serpent.
namaste	A very common word of greeting, often translated

as: 'I salute all divine qualities in you'.

Nandi — A bull, Shiva's vehicle and a symbol of fecundity.

Narayan — Vishnu represented as the creator of life.

nath — Literally, 'place'.

nirvana — Extinction of self, the goal of meditation.

P

panchayat — The old government system consisting of elected councils at local, regional and national levels.

Parvati — Shiva's consort, displaying both serene and fearful aspects.

pashmina — A shawl or blanket made of fine goat's wool.

Pashupati — Shiva in his aspect as 'Lord of the Beasts'. Symbolized by the *lingum*, he is believed to bring fecundity.

path — A small raised platform which provides shelter for travellers on important routes and intersections.

paubha — Traditional Newari painting, usually religious in motif.

pokhari — A large tank.

Pousch — The ninth month of the Nepalese year.

puja — Ritual offerings to the gods.

R

rakshi — A homemade wheat or rice liquor.

Rama — The seventh incarnation of Vishnu. A prince of the *Ramayana* epic.

Ramayana — The most widely known Hindu legend, in which Rama, with the aid of Hanuman and Garuda, rescues his wife, Sita, from the demon king Rawana.

Rawana — The anti-hero of the *Ramayana*.

rimpoche — The abbot of a Tibetan Buddhist monastery.

S

sadhu — A Hindu mendicant.

sanyasin — A religious ascetic who has renounced his ties to society.

Saraswati — Brahma's consort, worshipped in Nepal as the Hindu goddess of learning.

satal — A pilgrim's house.

shakti — Shiva's consort. Literally, the dynamic element in the male-female relationship, and the female aspect of the Tantric Absolute.

shikhara — A brick or stone temple of geometrical shape with a tall central spire.

Shitala Mai — A former ogress who became protector of children, worshipped at Swayambhunath.

Shiva — The most awesome of Hindu gods. He destroys all things, good as well as evil, allowing new creation to take shape.

Sita — Rama's wife, heroine of the *Ramayana* epic.

Srawan — The fourth month of the Nepalese year.

stupa — A bell-shaped relic chamber.

sundhara — A fountain with a golden spout.

Surjya — The sun god, often identified with Vishnu.

suttee — Former practise of immolating widows on their husband's funeral pyres.

T – U

Taleju Bhawani — The Nepalese goddess, originally a South Indian deity; an aspect of Devi.

Tara — Historically a Nepalese princess now deified by Buddhists and Hindus.

Terai — The Nepalese lowland region.

thangka	Religious scroll painting.
tika	A vermilion powder applied by Hindus to the forehead as a symbol of the presence of the divine.
tol	A street.
topi	Traditional Nepalese cap.
torana	Decorative carved crest over the door of a sanctum, with the figure of the deity at its center.

V – Z

vajra	In Tantric Buddhism, a ritual thunderbolt or curved sceptre symbolizing the Absolute. It also represents power and male energy (also *dorje*).
vihara	A Buddhist monastery, encompassing a *bahal* and a *bahil*.
Vishnu	One of the Hindu trinity, a god who preserves life and world itself. In Nepal, he is most commonly represented as Narayan.
yoni	A hole in a stone symbolizing the female sexual aspect. Usually seen together with a *lingum*.

ACKNOWLEDGMENTS

Cover, Houghton Mifflin ed	**T. Kelley/Apa Photo**
Cover, Apa, GeoCenter ed	**Bill Wassman**
Backcover	**John Cleare**
3, 4, 27, 28, 29, 31, 37, 39, 40, 43, 44, 46, 51, 55, 72, 75, 85T, 86T, 90, 92T, 93T	**Alain Evrard**
82	**Belinda Edwards**
47	**Craig Lovell**
26	**David Messent**
62	**Denise Tackett**
52	**Frances Klatzel**
33, 53, 54, 59, 65, 66, 67T, 68, 84T, 85B	**Galen Rowell**
78, 81, 83B	**Frances Higgins**
17, 87	**Jean Kugler**
61	**Jennifer Read**
35, 50, 69, 71, 80T, 88	**Jock Montogomery**
16	**Julian Cowan**
22	**K. Debnick**
43	**Kevin Bubriski**
14, 15, 19, 57, 79, 80B, 83T, 84B, 89	**Lisa Choegyal**
67B	**Nik Wheeler**
6, 43B	**Sanu Bajracharya**
34, 58, 70, 82	**Wendy Brewer Lama**
27T, 73, 74	**W.D. Andreae**
6/7	**Galen Rowell**
10/11	**Thomas Laird**
Handwriting	**V. Barl**
Maps	**Berndtson & Berndtson**
Cover Design	**Klaus Geisler**

Index

D, E

F

G

H

I, J, K

L

M

S

T

U, V

W, X, Z